ESCAPING A WELL OF FEAR

BY KRISTYN ANNE HUIGE

ACKNOWLEDGEMENTS

I would like to thank all of my friends and family for their support and help in the creation of this book. I would especially like to thank my children, Kurdt and Kelly Huige and Sara Huige. Thank you to my grandchildren, Alex, Anthony, Matthew, Dominic, Audra, Natalie, Christina, and Reece. You are all my pride and joy. Thank you for letting me tell your family story.

A special thank you to my sister Corrie and her husband, Chris Burgett, for their very special help and daily phone calls.

I am also grateful for my writing group for their help in composing this book. Linda Kurtz, Joel Thurtell, and Anne Lechartier…I could not have done this work without your help. You made this whole process exciting. Thank you.

Also, thank you to the Osher Lifelong Living Institute (University of Michigan senior activities program) for getting me started during COVID pandemic.

Thank you to neighbors who read, sometimes two versions, of my books: Susan Smereck and Patty and Brian Dillon. Thanks also to good friends who supported me when the going got tough. Elaine Hockman and the ladies' birthday group.

DEDICATION

This book is dedicated to my Mom. You are my hero. As a young person, I didn't fully appreciate what YOU had endured and the strength you displayed as you persevered. Thank you Mom.

Table of Contents

A DAY OF WAR

The dusty country road stretched ahead of us as we skipped to our temporary home after spending the day playing with the children in the neighboring farm. We spoke loudly to one another and occasionally launched into song. The air felt heavy with the afternoon summer heat. Suddenly, the loud noise of two planes overhead cut the stillness of the countryside.

My sisters and I (I was four years old, Corrie was two, and Ria was six) looked up to see two planes in deep descent aiming straight at us. I was terrified as I saw bullets hit the dirt. Pebbles and dust sprayed up and covered us. We froze in our steps.

"Run into the ditch," an old man behind us yelled. "Lie flat on the ground!"

When I heard his words, I grabbed Corrie's hand. We threw ourselves prone into the watery ditch alongside the road. The mud felt cold and squishy and my dress was now wet and dirty. Mama will be angry that I dirtied my dress. Crying, I looked up to see Ria dashing toward Mama as she screamed,

"Mama! Mamaaa!"

I wanted to do the very same thing and feel safety in Mama's arms, but I stayed where I was and squeezed my eyes shut, hoping that if I did not see what was happening, at least the noise would go away. I was terrified and I wondered what was going to happen. Then I heard a very loud explosion. Opening my eyes, I saw the large fireball. The strong smell of burning fuel and smoke filled the air. The second plane must have shot the other one down.

"They are dead! It's safe to come out now!" yelled the old man.

Corrie and I were safe for the moment. I shook and cried and felt that safety was not a condition of life I could count on. I had begun to feel less anxious with our time in the country, but now this experience once more shook me up. We ran to Mama. She was not mad at us for getting wet and dirty. She was relieved that we were not hurt. I was grateful that no one in our family was hurt. I will never forget the panic of this day. I believed I would die and I was grateful I survived. My life in Belgium was a series of similar days when life hung in the balance, but none were quite as terrifying. I was happy that I had Mama. She would see us through this war. I also began to believe that some part of me would know what to do when things got tough. I would learn and would know what to do. I would survive.

Who am I? I'm the girl who grabbed her little sister and dashed into the ditch. I'm Wilfrida Ferdinanda Louisa Huige, (now called Kristyn Anne Huige), born at the beginning of 1940 in my family's home on the Roomstraate in Lokeren, Belgium. I had thick, curly blond hair and green eyes, I loved to play. I was bright, stubborn, and energetic. I never ceased asking questions. I had a great talent for asking questions that did not have easy answers. I wanted the world to make sense. It did not. I expected the world around me to speak the truth...it did not.

MAMA AND OUR HOME

Who was this person who saw to it that the whole family survived World War II? Mama was probably the strongest woman I have ever met. I idolized her. She was tall and solidly built, with beautiful, long dark hair and expressive dark brown eyes. She always dressed fashionably, often with clothes she had designed and made herself. She was THE BOSS and no one questioned that. Words were not needed to communicate that you had done something wrong when she just glanced at you with her penetrating eyes. A glance was all that was needed, and you knew that you had to correct your behavior. Sounds tough, but once corrected, she didn't dwell on misdeeds, but she moved on and made it clear that you needed to do likewise. Her approach was the same when bad things happened…you just needed to be prepared to move on. I liked this approach to life, but it wasn't always as easy as.

She gave the most reassuring, wonderful hugs I have ever felt. She was more fun than any other adult I knew. Her raucous laugh would permeate the room and it was impossible not to join in the laughter. She always looked ready for company. She loved lavender and lilies of the valley and never missed applying one of these perfumes. I loved to sit near her and take in her wonderful aroma. She read to us, played our games, and even had tea parties with us. She was a bookkeeper, a seamstress, a wonderful baker and cook. She could make the tastiest soups and bread. My favorite bread was raisin, when we had raisins. It was particularly good when it was warm and WHEN we had butter…ooh so good! We didn't have butter very often.

Mama was definitely unique and a survivor. She had faith in herself and gave everyone around her the feeling that everything would be okay. She persevered in all things and when she had a problem, she pushed on until she came up with a solution. She would be the first to admit that she was very frightened in the war, but she would tell herself and us to keep on doing what we were doing, that things would be okay. She was brave and she carried on with life. She carried her body so erect and tall that no one would dare test her resolve. She was a force,

Mama lived through two world wars and looked after people in both of those stressful times. During World War I, her mother, burned her legs badly in a kitchen accident and was incapacitated for months. Mama, who was an eight-year-old child, looked after her, as Ooma was confined to her room. Ooma had a major emotional breakdown at this time and the doctor who was treating her yelled at eight-year-old Stella for not moving her mother into the living room so she could be around people.

"Stupid girl...your mother needs the stimulation of others! Don't you know any better?"

This was during World War I and Mama was also looking after her two younger brothers, four and six years old. With her papa gone a good deal of the time, Stella could barely keep up with tending the house and the younger children, and had no idea what her mama needed to be happy. She didn't even know what that meant. "If I had only known what to do. I just didn't know what to do. I didn't know how to take care of my Mama."

I believe that this guilt plagued her the rest of her life. She felt as though she could never do enough.

In World War II, Mama had four children and her extended family to protect. She did so with an unbelievable ferocity. How she managed to protect four children who were American citizens living in German-occupied Belgium is still a mystery to me. I wonder how she kept us safe from the German army which occupied our town and our house. We lived with German soldiers for the duration of the war. Mama saved our lives and I am grateful. Despite all the responsibilities she had taken on, she still managed to maintain the merry twinkle in her eyes and to fully appreciate a joke or a funny situation. She was fun. Her laughter filled the room. We loved to hear her laugh. Although fear was our constant companion, Mama's laugh grounded us and lessened our fears.

Mama married Papa before the war began in something of an arranged marriage. Oom Charles and Tante Louise arranged for them to meet as Mama "wasn't getting any younger." Papa had a twelve-year-old son who needed a mother and it would also be a good match for Papa. He had immigrated to the United States from the Netherlands at age eighteen and became a naturalized citizen. He was the second oldest of a family with seventeen children, and he was irresponsible. In fact, the story I heard was that his family had given him a one-way ticket to the United States after he had managed to lose a truckload of meat while he was drinking in a bar. In the United States he had married and begun a family with the birth of his son Johnnie. He had also started an independent business which was doing quite well. His wife died and he was left with the child to raise. He was depressed and felt overwhelmed with the tasks involved with caring for a young child and a business. He sold the business and decided to go home to the Netherlands and ask his family for help.

Papa returned to the family in the Netherlands in 1935 for support and to possibly find a wife. He met Mama and so, after three dates, they married.

Mama thought Papa was fat and Ooma said, "Have you looked at yourself lately? You're not so skinny."

The marriage was one of convenience, not love. When the war began, Papa left Belgium to go to Spain in the hope that the war would be short lived. He chose to go back to the United States after it became clear to him that the war would not be of short duration. I was almost one year old.

I had no early memories of Papa but I certainly created a multitude of fantasies about him. My sisters joined in the dramas we created about Papa. We had our very own superhero and decided he would swoop in and rescue us if we felt in danger. When we saw the planes overhead, we imagined Papa was there to force the enemy to leave us alone. I even created stories of Papa, the pilot, who would rescue us by shooting down planes that threatened us.

"Those are my girls on the road. I'm going to shoot that plane down and save them."

We talked about him, made up stories, and built him up in our minds to be the most wonderful, bravest person who ever existed. We prayed and prayed for Papa to come home safely. We continued to pray even after the war, when we did not understand where Papa was and why he did not come home. My first memory of him was when I was seven years old.

Papa and Mama settled in a large three-story home on a lovely cobblestone street in Lokeren. We loved the cobblestones, but as the war went on, there were more and more areas where the stones were broken up due to bombings. Lokeren was a small town not far from

Antwerp. Our house had both a front door and a large entryway for cars which was all marble. The entry for cars had an old car sitting there that never moved. Mama had a storefront business on the main floor which she turned into a dressmaker's shop. We loved playing with the mannequins, sewing machines, and clothes, but we were a nuisance for Mama in her shop. Behind the shop on the main floor was a large kitchen with a coal stove which was our main source of heat. In the winter, we all dressed around the stove in the mornings as it was the only warm place in the house. I loved my room which was on the third floor and had windows that looked out on the backyard…my favorite place. I didn't like sleeping there by myself, as I was afraid at night and wanted to sleep with someone. I often slept with Marieke, a woman who worked with Mama, or with my sisters. Marieke didn't seem to mind sleeping with me, even though I had nightmares, screamed and woke her up many times during the night.

Dressing in the mornings was sometimes a battle, especially when the weather was quite cold.

"It's my turn to be closer to the stove, you were closest yesterday, Ria. Mamaaa, Ria is hogging the warm spot by the stove and it's my turn."

The kitchen had running water but no refrigerator. We had an icebox. That means that ice was what kept our food cold. Ice, however, was scarce during the war, so we just kept our food out on the kitchen counter and saw to it that there were few leftovers. We were told that the food that was left had to be boiled to kill the bacteria so we wouldn't get sick. Mama shopped every day for the food we would eat that night, as long as the shops were open and there was no bombing. Some of the food we ate came from our garden, that is, if the German soldiers didn't take it. They were frequently coming into the house and taking what they wanted, especially food. Mama cooked on the big coal stove which dominated the kitchen. I loved spending time in the kitchen. It always smelled very good and I could always count on the tastes I got from Mama or Marieke to be absolutely wonderful. I still remember some of my favorite foods: hache, huttseput, oliebollen, raisin bread, and all of Mama's great soups. Mama's cooking always tasted wonderful. Once a month, we would get a piece of candy which was so sour that we made the most outrageous faces when we sucked on it. I think we called them "moeillitrekkors" meaning "bad face makers." We didn't have sugar, so we did what we could without it. I do not recall missing sweets as we had never had them from the time I was born. Mama was a champion bread maker and the aroma would bathe the house.

We ate very little meat as it was not readily available. Occasionally, Mama would buy some meat on what she whispered was the "black market."

I whispered back, "It doesn't look black to me. It looks red."

Everyone in the room laughed and I felt confused.

Mama said: "Don't worry about it, it is just regular meat…Okay?"

There were many foods we just could not get. We didn't miss them as we had never tasted these foods. There was little or no butter, cheese, meat, and fruits. Mama sometimes described these mystery foods and included tasty descriptions of her favorites. Here was another reason for the war to end. We really wanted to try these wonderful things as they sounded yummy.

Our bedrooms were quite large and everyone had a wash basin which often froze in the winter, but at least we could break the ice and wash our faces. It was a quick way to wake up. We also had chamber pots by the bed in case we needed to pee at night. The front of the home was stone, with a large covered drive-through area for a car. The car, parked by the front entry, was not used for the duration of the war as no one could drive and there was no gas.

As one entered the house, the first thing to see was a huge statue of a naked Venus de Milo with no arms, and a large circular marble staircase. As children, my friends and I did spend time giggling over the statue. She was a topic for all of the neighborhood kids mainly because she was naked. She was bigger than Mama. Mama was unhappy about having such a "vulgar" statue in the entry of her home. She did not believe that Venus spoke well for us when it came to visitors. I loved Venus and at times, we all tried to put clothes and drapes on her. We included her in our play, where she would sometimes be a giant who would make the German soldiers behave.

"Captain Venus, what is the plan to rid us of this army that is attacking us?"

"Children, you need to keep fighting, don't cry, stay strong, and all will be well in time."

As the war continued, Venus was often the victim of bombings and lost some of her body parts when the house was bombed. She got some wounds to her head and lost part of her leg. We still thought she was beautiful. She was still there to protect our stairs and keep bad people away from us. Although we were told not to play on the stairs, they were so inviting that we often gave in to our desires and as was predicted by Mama, we did have a disaster. My little sister Corrie was playing with us and fell down the stairs. She was bleeding all over the place. She had to have stitches.

Venus made it clear that "you'd better listen to the grownups around you." We were more careful about the stairs after that.

My favorite part of the house was our wonderful backyard. The yard had stone walls that were probably six feet tall; at least, they seemed VERY tall to me. Even on my tiptoes, I couldn't begin to see over them. There were cobblestone terraces and a number of tall trees. We had some cages for rabbits and a huge vegetable garden. I loved the rabbits, but the rule was to leave them alone. I was drawn to the soft, cuddly creatures and would occasionally climb into the pen and pet them. Strangely, even though they kept having babies that grew up, the numbers remained the same. I found out later that some of the wonderful stews we had were courtesy of the rabbits. I was very angry and sad to learn that they had been killed for food; however, I'm glad I didn't know this information at the time. I would probably have thrown up if I had known that I was actually eating one of my furry friends.

Mama definitely had a green thumb. We helped her plant seeds and then watched daily as the sprouts grew into the food we would eat. We played all kinds of games and had many celebrations in our garden. It felt like a safe spot for me in the midst of chaos, a place where I could shut out the noise of the frightening world. I think my sisters felt the same way. It was my quiet, magical place where I could escape the war. It was a place where Mama seemed more relaxed and could have fun with us. It was in the garden that she told us stories, read to us, and play our games with us. I fondly remember Mama and Marieke playing ring-around-the-rosy with us. I especially remember all of us falling down shrieking and laughing with abandon.

The garden was also a place where we could usually talk a bit more freely and ask questions. "Why is there a war? Who is bombing us? Why don't they like us?

When will it stop?" *I begged for answers but just managed to annoy the grownups.*

Mama tried to answer our questions, but I don't think we understood her responses. I wanted to know more.

"I know we are in a war, but I do not understand why we are here and why our family just did not leave the country when Papa did. Papa left, why not us? Why did the Germans hate my friend Annie's family so much that they bombed her house and killed her Papa? Would they do that to us also?"

Mama said, "I know this is very hard on all of us. I don't really understand why all of this is happening. It's complicated for me, and I have no idea how to explain war to you. When you get older, you might have a better understanding of what causes wars. For the moment, we need to take care of ourselves and believe that all of this will have an ending."

There always seemed to be a grownup around who was available to talk to us or hug us. We generally had a lot of family living with us. In the garden, it felt like we were never alone. We didn't feel lonely. We felt taken care of. It was the world outside of the garden that was dangerous. When we were out on the street we rushed to get to our destination. We avoided looking at the German soldiers on the street and we especially did not look into their eyes.

Mama said, "Just look away. Don't give them any reason to suspect us or be angry with us."

So, while on the street, we held hands and rushed. I expected that, any moment, a bomb would fall on us and crush us.

The only place, other than our garden, where I felt safe was our church with its starry ceiling and many statues of angels and God. I believed that no one, no matter how evil, would hurt God's home. Also, it was clear to me that Mama felt the same way I did since she seemed much more relaxed when she sat down to pray. We were both wrong in believing bombs would not fall on the church, as even the church had damage. Mama was always a very spiritual person. When she experienced a dilemma, she prayed to God and to a saint, especially St. Joseph, and she generally found a way out of her problem. She went to church as often as she could, and took us with her whenever possible. Ooma and Oopa and my Ooms and Tante didn't seem as interested in God as Mama. Ooma and Oopa had trouble walking any distance and they felt church was too far away. Mama wouldn't miss mass, no matter what was going on. I think she would have willingly gone even during a bombing.

Mama really believed God would save us. Her faith was beautiful and was an integral part of her until she died at age eighty-two. She saw to it that no matter what was going on in her world, God came first. She would make it to mass. She loved meeting with her women friends during and after church and loved all of the fellowship times, although there were less and less of them as the war dragged on. Most important of all, Mama prayed for Papa to return to us and that we would all survive the war.

When Mama closed her business, we had Mama all to ourselves. We didn't have to share her with work. We continued to also have Marieke, so it felt like we had two Mamas. I don't know what we did for money throughout the war, but we survived.

I worried that Marieke would go back to her family if Mama couldn't pay her, but she said, "Don't worry about that…I won't leave you." She did not leave us and that felt good.

All the adults' reassurances, however, could not block out the noise and chaos of war. I remember bombings and destruction and soldiers and parades and listening in silence for the high-pitched whistle of the bomb that was falling to end. I wondered, where would it fall? There was one particular bomb that we either had to hear the whistle until the end or it was better if we did not hear it. I didn't understand which was good or which was bad. I felt confused about this.

We were all very quiet in the air raid shelter. Even though the place was filled with parents and children, I could have heard a pin drop as I waited for that whistle to end. The air raid sirens terrified me too. They wailed and wailed and it seemed they would never stop. As I think about this now, I feel my body tense up, sense the tears in my eyes, and swallow hard. As much as I have spoken about this, I still feel overwhelmed by these feelings. There were many times when I thought the bombing would go on forever. I cried silent tears through the violent sounds of the world breaking apart. I believed that making noise would just increase my vulnerability. I learned to be quiet…to close my eyes and hope that if I saw nothing, then nothing would happen. I think that we all learned to keep our sounds inside of us. We all learned silence.

My body and my mind ached from holding myself tightly. Even after the war was over, my muscles felt as though they never came to terms with the peacetime world. My body feels rigid. As a child, I was afraid of walking around the town and seeing houses destroyed. I was frightened when I saw injured people and I prayed I wouldn't get hurt and especially that Mama would not get hurt or die. I don't believe I ever got used to seeing the damage to people suffered. Our home had some damage and many broken windows. I got something in my eye that scratched the cornea so badly that the doctor told Mama that I was blind in my right eye. It was probably a piece of shrapnel. I had to wear a black patch for several years.

We were fortunate that we had a large basement that provided some safety during bombings.

I asked Mama, "Why are basements safe places to be during bombings when the whole house could fall into the basement?"

I was worried about bringing this thought up to Mama as I feared I would make her more afraid than she already was. I asked her anyway.

Mama said, "The walls of the basement are very strong and there are no windows to break and cut people."

Everything was so confusing. I did not want Mama afraid. I watched her very carefully. If she looked afraid, I knew things were really bad.

I was confused. Nothing really made sense to me. Loving people were suddenly in a rage when certain topics I did not understand were discussed. Everybody was tense. I wanted to know why people did bad things to others. I tried talking to God about this. He didn't answer me. One confusing day rolled into the next confusing day.

Mama said, "Don't try to make sense of this."

I continued to try in spite of Mama's advice. It seemed as though there was nothing I could control, and I felt afraid. My greatest fear was that something would happen to Mama. She was my rock. We sheltered both in our basement and in the larger shelter with our neighbors. Fear became central to our way of life and accompanied even the simplest of our life experiences. When all was black in the night I would wake and jump at the slightest noise. In blackness it was impossible to see the enemy, to make out who made the noise, to see which direction I needed to be alert for. I wanted light, and it wasn't there at night. Some nights, when there were blackouts, it was very dark in our home. We would cover all of our windows and Mama said that the German flyers couldn't see us at night if all was dark. Days were easier for me, as I could see and identify the dangers that would come my way.

My nightmares continue to this day. My night screams seem to have no end and no amount of insight smothers the flames of what I believe to be my very early experiences. My younger sister and I decided to write about our war experiences and many of them have come alive again for us. The more we have bathed these experiences with light, the more healing has come to us. I've tried to come to terms with the war years but my struggle continues. I was convinced that if I could make some sense out of my experiences my fear would dissipate if I could only understand what was going on.

SCHOOL AND OTHER LESSONS

Our school in Belgium was a fast walk down our street. Girls always dressed in their best dresses and we had big bows in our hair. I think our parents tried to keep up appearances so that we would be less afraid of the changes in our lives. My teacher had dark hair, kept every hair in place, tightly in a bun. I no longer remember her name but I can still clearly see her face in my mind. She was firm, but she had probably twenty children in her charge all between two and four years of age. We had desks and were learning to read and count. I can still remember feeling proud and powerful just sitting at my desk. To have a book in front of me and to understand numbers was a thrill I felt every day I sat in that seat. We were all traumatized, however, and we jumped, cried out, or started to cry with any sound out of the ordinary. If a book dropped, it felt like the end of the world to some of us. In spite of what was happening in the world around me, I love school!

Several of the children in my class were so scared that they would occasionally pee in their seats. I don't believe I remember any punishments or teasing, but the teacher managed to take care of these problems. We were children in fear...fearful of leaving our homes…fearful when our parents left us at school…fearful of what we might find when we got home.

We wondered, would our mothers and fathers still be there? Would they be dead? This was a universal fear, even though we had no idea what death meant. There seemed to always be someone who lost an important person. We prayed that it wouldn't happen to us.

"What was death anyway?" My childish imagination painted elaborate, ghoulish images that terrified me as I pondered this question. "What happens when a person dies? Does the ghost go to heaven with Jesus? What happens to the body?"

Mama said Papa's youngest brother died at the beginning of the war.

"Where did he go? Why does God let us die?"

The answer adults gave to this question was generally, "Oh, don't think about that. Let me tell you a story."

They would proceed with a story that completely changed the subject and did not satisfy me. I could see, though, that the other children felt better. But I did not feel satisfied.

As a very small child, I worried about disappearing. I worried that if I died, I would just disappear. I had known some people who died and they did just disappear…poof! Mama seemed confused about how to talk with me about this. I knew I did not want to disappear. I desperately wanted people to remember me. If I died in a bombing, something about me had to stay alive. Mama said I would always be alive in her heart, just as she would be alive in my heart if she died. That did not satisfy me. It was not enough. I decided I would need to do something so wonderful that people would remember me. Now, my task was to discover what I could do that would be so wonderful. In many, many ways, I was way too young to persevere on this issue, yet it took over my thoughts. I thought, maybe I'll be a painter. I could paint, but not like the artists our teacher talked about. This issue continued.

At one time, we had terrible floods in town and we could not get home. I was worried that we would be stuck in school. Lots of Papas from the town came to the school and took their children on their shoulders to their homes or a shelter. We worried that no one would take us since our Papa was not around, but we felt relief when some of the other Papas took us, too.

"Yea…it is so much fun riding on Hannah's Papa's shoulders."

When we arrived home, Mama warned us, "Don't go to the basement; it's dangerous because of all of the water. We are flooded."

Of course, we only had to hear that there was something going on in the basement for us to head that direction. "Mama, the potatoes and apples are swimming in the basement. It is so funny. Look at all of the stuff…and it really stinks too."

Mama didn't think it was very funny and she was about to admonish us for disobeying her when she looked at the mess we were laughing about and suddenly, she joined us in the laughter when she saw the apples, potatoes, turnips and a whole garden full of vegetables bobbing and dancing around in the water. It was like "the dance of the vegetables". When the laughter was over, we saw that the water was muddy and was almost to the top step. It looked very deep and dangerous. Mama again warned us of the danger, and we listened to her and obeyed. We were grateful that it receded quickly and then we only had a big clean-up to do. I couldn't believe all of the mud we had to get rid of in the basement. "Yuck."

My sisters and I talked a lot about the flood and the way our friends' families helped us. We took this caring to heart and loved the attention, especially from the Papas. At these times of stress, we sorely missed having a Papa around, and I believe Mama really missed having someone to support her. She continually prayed to St. Joseph that she would hear from Papa, but we heard nothing.

As we prayed, we were aware that we had no idea who we were praying for. I know that I could not remember Papa, and besides was born about eight months after Papa left Belgium. Ria and I were just too young to have memories of him.

Mama showed us pictures and that helped us form an image, but to us, he was a stranger. At times, we imagined a superhero type of person who would make everything alright. We made up stories about Papa and tried to bring him into our life. He became this handsome person who could solve any problem that could befall us. Perhaps he could even solve problems that Mama could not. Maybe he could stop the war. We tried to bring him to life in our own way. We spent a good deal of time pretending and creating stories about a Papa we did not know.

"General Papa, what will you do to stop the bombing in our town?"

As he towered over us, he would say, "I will tell them to stop destroying this town and scaring children or they will be really sorry." We truly believed he had the power to make our problems go away. He would bring peace.

I loved it when Mama talked about peace. She said it was a time when people got along and didn't fight. There were no bombings and people weren't getting hurt.

Marieke looked after us while Mama worked as a dressmaker. Very few people bought new clothes, so the business didn't bring in much money. We were so happy that Marieke decided to stay with us, even though Mama was unable to pay her when her business closed. She was warm, loving, had great hugs and was also a lot of fun. She had curly brown hair and a funny snaggletooth in the front of her mouth. What I loved the most was her wonderful smile which could light up any room. She lived with us at the house and was like a member of the family. She was like a second Mama. She had a boyfriend, and when she was going to go out with him, she would dress up and put make-up on. We were fascinated. She ended her preparation by drawing a brown line up the backs of the calves of her legs. She laughed and said that this was cheaper than nylons which apparently could not be found in stores and no one had the money to buy them anyway. Her boyfriend was the man who sold coal throughout our town. He was a big, friendly person who often entered into our play with Marieke. Our family always felt a bit more complete when they were both with us.

I was the middle child, and since I was born at the beginning of 1940, I was considered the person who "brought in the war." I was always a bit confused by this, but was consistently assured that the war was not my fault. The statement did, however, feed my secretly held sense of power and guilt. I became the child who would walk into the room where there was conflict and instantly apologize for whatever the problem might be. I think I grew to believe that it is much easier to stop conflict by saying "I did it" and "I'm sorry," and hopefully the chaos and noise would end. It often did end, solidifying my belief system. It amazes me how early I began to etch out the design for my life. It took very few words, whether said in anger or jest or love, for me to latch on and make life decisions that often directed the path of my life. For me, chaos, noise, feelings, and silence were all to be feared and avoided. These are very difficult to avoid during a time of war. They are also difficult to avoid during peacetime. Strangely, the relative silence after the war was as disconcerting to me as the war itself. I kept waiting for the "bombs" to fall. At times I even produced the "bombs" that I was expecting in a desperate attempt at mastery over my thoughts and feelings.

A HOUSE FULL OF FAMILY…AND SOLDIERS

My early memories are of bombing…military parades down our street… strangers in our home. The regular people in my home were Mama, Ria, Marieke, Corrie, Johnnie and me. Johnnie, my half-brother from Papa's first marriage, was probably fifteen by the time I was born. Other were the German soldiers and officers who were billeted in our home. The SS soldiers were scary and we had to be very careful about saying anything when they were around. We even had to be careful about whispering when they were home because they would get angry and yell out: "What's going on?" We would usually answer "nothing" or even "we were asking about dinner."

Mama said, "The best thing to say is nothing because they can enter the room at any time." Saying nothing was always very hard for me. It seems I always had something I wanted to say, but I tried to be good and stay silent.

Papa, being an American citizen, had been warned that he would probably soon become a prisoner of war if he did not leave. Johnnie, though also an American, stayed behind and blended in as a Belgian. This was difficult for him as English was his native language and I was told he spoke Flemish with a bit of an American accent. He chose to generally remain silent. While Johnnie was with us, he spent a great deal of time with the Belgian underground and we have grown to believe that's why he had to leave precipitously. One day, he was with us and then he was gone. He apparently got word that he was to be arrested and fled to Spain. Somewhere along the way, he joined the American army and ended up in the South Pacific war. Being an American was a scary thing to be.

We didn't see Papa again until 1947 and then it was just briefly, as he said he had to return to the United States to prepare a home for us since he wanted us to live in America. I do wish I had gotten to know both Papa and Johnnie better. The coming and going of people in our lives, with no explanations, compounded the pain of loss and made getting into intimate relations problematic for all of us. Even as a child, I held back giving my heart to anyone, as I could be abandoned at any time.

I got used to turmoil and change. German soldiers lived in our home, resulting in many whispered conversations and hovering around the secret radio with someone watching to make sure the area was safe. News from the outside world was scarce but valued by the adults around us. I have no idea who brought the radio in the house, but I guessed it might have been Johnnie. He always seemed to have news about the war. As a child, I did not understand what the adults were doing. I pretended to understand the radio so that I could be part of the secret society that understood what was happening. I knew there was a war and that this was not the way that people should live. However, war was all I knew and I could not imagine what "no war" felt or looked like. At times, I thought that maybe I could play a game called "no war," but I could never imagine how to start or even talk about this game. When I played tag, I knew that when I was "it," I had to chase the others and make someone else "it," and when I was not "it," I had to run to keep from getting touched so that I would not become "it." It was all pretty simple. Life was not that simple, although I often wished it were. I had not experienced a day when we were not ready to run for safety at any time. I needed to be alert at all times.

Some of the soldiers the "good people" in my life were trying to avoid were often kind to me and even played with me. I would play ball or other games and some of the young soldiers were even nicer to me than my brother. I understood why everyone stopped talking when a Nazi soldier would enter a room; even the grownups avoided trouble. I was afraid that I would speak out and break the silence with something "bad" and get everyone in trouble. Sometimes, when we were playing with a soldier, Mama would call us away as though what we were doing was bad. Relationships outside the family were definitely confusing. It was hard to think of "bad" and "good" people. There were, however, many soldiers who I had no trouble thinking of as "bad" because they treated my family badly. They yelled and made demands and it was clear that Mama was afraid of them.

Throughout a good portion of the war, my uncles, aunt, grandparents, and cousin Ria lived with us as our home was large and safer than family homes in Antwerp. I enjoyed having a houseful of people around. My Ooma and Oopa were quite old and I had to be careful around them so they would not fall. They were fearful and angry about the war. Oopa was generally quiet and said very little. He was a small man and had been a train conductor for most of his adult life until the beginning of the war. He seemed to have trouble with the lack of things to do. He seemed agitated, but he never complained. Ooma was a small woman who was bent over and had back pain. She said very little but her eyes spoke volumes. They were large and very sad. There were lines around the outside of her eyes that Mama called laugh lines. So I guess that at one time she smiled a lot. You knew when she was not pleased and she reinforced her displeasure with a painful pinch. Despite the pinching, I knew that Ooma loved me and that she only pinched to get our attention. It was also clear to me that Mama really loved her parents and that she would do anything for them. I loved to watch them talk to each other and do things together.

Mama felt concerned about how to look after her parents, and how to protect them from the chaos of children. Now, with the addition of cousin Ria, there were four little girls around. The activity and noise levels were definitely something to contend with. My uncles and Tante Rie were very mild-mannered and quiet but tolerated the noise of children and no one complained. Mama and Marieke joined in our noise at every opportunity and I admit, I did feel safer and more secure when they did. Having grown-ups around who were consistently fearful made me afraid, but having the two most important adults play with us diminished the fear.

Even though war was the backdrop of my life, there was some routine which I learned to count on. School was my favorite routine. This involved learning, reading, playing with friends, and relating with people outside of my immediate family. There were strict rules about school, though: someone took you to school in the morning and you came home immediately after school. No after-school play at friends' homes. At some point, the bombing became too dangerous and our town and street had been hit badly. School closed down. It was more and more risky to be in our town.

One day, while we were being bombed, Mama rushed us to the basement, only to discover that Corrie was not there. We all panicked as we were not allowed to leave the shelter during the bombing. We had to wait to look for her.

"Where is Corrie? Is she hurt? Will we find her?"

We heard a number of large bombs land and we could hear the crystal sound of many windows breaking. As soon as we could, we dashed upstairs and found Corrie in one of the upstairs bedrooms screaming "booma, booma, booma" and pointing to the sky. She was fine and seemed unaware of the danger she had been in.

Several nuns at our school had died in one of the blasts. We were all sad. Our teachers and the other school nuns were very sad. Shortly after this bombing, we sought refuge in the countryside.

A REFUGE THAT WASN'T

We packed a few belongings, one favorite toy each. I chose my doll, Corrie chose her ball, and Ria took a book. We could only take what we could carry. We proceeded on foot to the safety of the countryside. It was a long, tiring, and dusty journey. We were hot and our feet hurt. The country was a world we had no experience with. There were woods, pastures, and fields the farmers had planted with various crops. We saw many cows, sheep, horses, pigs, and other animals we could not name, and we were thrilled each time we saw a different animal. We saw farmers busy in their fields. I was surprised that there were so few houses and that the houses often had large barns and other buildings next to them. Mama talked to us throughout the trip and told us about the farms and animals we saw. I was surprised she knew so much about farms and animals. I was aware, however, that Mama was afraid, even though she told me that she was not. I decided that I needed to keep an eye on her. Maybe I could help her.

I had no idea where we were going and how the war would be at the end of our journey. "Do they have war where we are going? Are there bombings and soldiers there? What will happen to Ooma and Oopa? Are they going to Antwerp? Are they safe? Will we see them again? Do they have food?" The questions poured out of us, as did our tears and fears. Mama walked to the side of the road and we followed. She took us in her arms and softly addressed our fears.

"Yes, the war is also in Antwerp but at least Ooma and Oopa will have food…more food than we had in Lokeren. They will stay in their home and family will look after them. Don't worry. We will all have more safety and more food." I didn't realize that Mama had been worried about food. I thought we had enough. We felt better after Mama's talk and hugs and again joined the people walking on the road.

We finally reached our destination after a day of walking. Marieke had some family members who were farmers who agreed to take us in. Mama insisted on working in the fields, baling hay to earn our keep, even though she had never done this kind of work before. I still remember her bloody hands at the close of each workday. She never complained. We all slept on pallets on the floor, but we felt safe. We played with the farmer's children, even though they said they didn't want us there, and tried to stay out of trouble. Play with these children often ended with tears for us, as we were a lot younger and not as fast. We played hide-and-seek and discovered many very dirty places on the farm. One game involved the big boy from the farm playing keep-away with my dolly. He threw it in the outside toilet and I cried and cried. It was gone. It was as though I had lost my best friend.

I've already recounted the most painful memory I have of this time, but I feel a need to repeat it with more detail as I am reminiscing about my past. My sisters and I were walking down the dirt road to the house we were living in. It was a beautiful summer day. The sky was blue with fluffy clouds and a slight breeze. I could hear the birds chirping in the trees, the cows mooing in the pasture, and an occasional neigh from the horses. We were talking loudly, then softly, and then singing as we strolled home. Suddenly, the silence was broken by the loud engines of two planes. On looking up, we saw that they were swooping down towards us. One of the planes started strafing the road. I could see the bullets pick up dirt and pebbles from the road in front of us. For a moment, I froze in terror. Then I grabbed Corrie's hand as a man on the road said, "Jump in the ditch. " We quickly obeyed and threw ourselves in the culvert partly filled with water and hugged the ground. Ria was panic-stricken and ran screaming down the road, waving her arms at Mama. I knew she needed to take cover. I was helpless when it came to reaching her with my screams. She heard nothing. She was so upset I believe she only heard the sounds of the planes and of her heart thumping in her chest. As I saw her running towards Mama, I desperately wanted to be there with Mama, but I knew that would not be a good thing to do. I felt jealous of my sister that she was with Mama, my safe place. Thankfully, she was not physically hurt, but I am sure this memory stayed with her as it did with all of us. I remember screaming for her to join us, but I'm sure she did not hear me. When the plane that had shot at us started to go up again, the other plane, which had been behind the first one, shot the German plane down. We heard a very loud explosion and saw the plane crash a short distance ahead of us. We saw and smelled the fire it started. We were later told that the German pilot was dead. Lying down in the weeds and water on the roadside with my little sister, I was shaking and felt incredibly cold. Corrie and I reached for each other and hugged each other for dear life. We were both trembling, but we also knew we were both alive and not hurt. Our small island of safety in the country had been breached. We climbed out of our watery refuge and ran, dripping, to Mama and felt the safety of her enveloping us with her arms. I was happy that she wasn't angry at us for messing our clothes. None of us ever spoke about our narrow escape from danger.

Easygoing walks down the road were now avoided. We did, however, take occasional trips to the wreck of the plane. We seemed obsessed with gawking at what remained of the plane. It was as though we kept letting ourselves know that a very bad thing had happened but we were still alive. We were not physically hurt. We survived and the bad man from the plane died. We stayed close to the farmhouse. After several more months, we returned to our home in Lokeren. We were now aware that there was also war in the countryside. Could we find safety walking home? What would we find?

GOING HOME AGAIN TO A CHANGED CITY

Going back home was hard as I saw the damage that the bombings had done to my town. Some places were just piles of rocks, glass, personal possessions, furniture, and even toys. Photos and papers decorated the landscape. I felt myself stiffen as panic gripped me. I glanced at Mama but she just looked ahead and kept walking. I decided that Mama was right: not seeing the destruction was probably the best solution. However, I couldn't "not look." I took it all in. Lokeren didn't look like Lokeren anymore. I couldn't believe the destruction. I convinced myself that my home would be rubble, but we were one of the fortunate families. Our home had many broken windows, but most of it was still standing. We cleaned up and got on with life as usual. It became more difficult to tell what life as usual was, but we continued looking for the security that school, reading, games, music, and other familiar activities provided in our lives. I became acutely aware of feeling very tired. It was as though I was on that long march in the country over and over again. I felt very weary of the war, as I am sure everyone was. I had more and more trouble sleeping. I would doze off and wake up in a nightmare. Sleeplessness, nightmares, and fatigue became part of everyday life.

We went to church and thanked God that we were still alive. I loved that church and still remember how huge and powerful it felt to me. The pulpit rose way above the congregation and consisted of beautiful wood and carvings of angels. It was a very dark wood and Corrie sometimes crawled on the wood and nestled amongst the angels. The church always felt empty to me, as fewer and fewer people seemed to attend. The building's ceiling was a dark color, probably blue, and was covered with a myriad of little stars. I remember many days at church services where all that my sisters and I did was sit back and stare at the ceiling. In fact, when my sisters and I and my cousin Ria visited Lokeren and the church as adults, the first thing that all four of us did was look up to see if the stars were still there. They were and we had a sense that all was really right with the world.

The church also provided times to celebrate. Many of the saints' days were times to have parades and to party. During those days, we could put the war aside. Our favorite day for parades was St. Niklaas, when St. Nicolas and Swarte Piet were the prime characters. Swarte Piet (Black Pete) was a man who blackened his face with coal dust and had a huge sack to carry away bad children. I remember how all the children were terrified of Swarte Piet and his very large sack. We were all so frightened of him that most of us never looked to see what he actually did with this sack. Most of my images of Swarte Piet were made up in my mind. On St. Niklaas day, we would put our shoes out and pray that St. Niklaas would leave us a present or some candy. We all hid when Swarte Piet came by in the parade because we were not sure if we had been bad, and we came out when it was safe. (This was also the closest I came to seeing what was purported to be a "black person" until I came to the United States.) The other days that had memorable celebrations were Christmas Eve and Day. We, of course, had a parade, and then we had some special food at home, and best of all, we all got an orange as a present. These were days when we could put the war out of our minds for a few hours and focus on fun. Easter was also one of these special days and we did often get a special piece of candy.

We cherished these days. Presents of toys, which we discovered later, were not part of these celebrations.

Mama relied on religion as her sustenance. She prayed constantly that Papa would return to us safely. We heard nothing from him and we prayed that he was still alive. We could not remember this person we prayed for. We were all so young and our thoughts were weighed down by fears that we would not survive. Papa was this mysterious person who held a primary place in our family. It was almost like all would be well when he appeared. Mama prayed to St. Joseph every day and especially on his feast day. She believed, and I believed, that God would set things right. God would bring my Papa back and then everything would be alright. Our mystery Papa would bring order to the world. Sometime after the war was over, she finally heard from him on St. Joseph's feast day.

The stress of the war affected all of us differently. I all tended to be nervous and jumpy. None of us had an easy time sleeping and we took turns sleeping with Mama and Marieke. I had issues with bedwetting and then had to deal with shame. We preferred to stay at home and not go to the homes of friends or family. We worried that if we went to a friend, there might be a bombing and our family at home would die. Fear of being left alone in the world plagued our days. Our immune systems were weakened by this stress and by the lack of some basic foods such as meats, milk, and fruit and we tended to get sick easily.

I tended to have injuries like the one to my eye and stomach aches. I felt embarrassed wearing the black eye patch and was often teased by my friends. It's unclear to me how the injury happened but I sustained a large scar over the cornea. Mama said it could have happened during a bombing but I was unclear. This injury resulted in many trips to Antwerp and Brussels to see specialists. It was thought that I was blind in my right eye and we feared it could be permanent. My vision was also threatened when we all got the measles. My eyes were covered for several weeks. When we were getting better, Mama had a rare treat for us...oranges! We were thrilled. All of a sudden, I piped up, *"This isn't an orange; mine is red."* I was peaking under my blindfold. Mama cried with joy and explained that it was a different kind of orange but that I could have whatever color I wanted as long as I could see. We were all grateful that my vision was no longer threatened. However, because of my eye problems, ironically, I did see more of the war than my sisters.

On several trips to see eye doctors, Mama and I crossed the border into the Netherlands and visited Papa's family. We went to the farm where he was born and met some of his sixteen brothers and sisters. I couldn't believe how big his family was and it was wonderful meeting so many people who were family. One of his young brothers had died at the beginning of the war. When I went on these trips, Mama would usually smuggle some food home, as Opa Huige always had some wonderful meats to share. Mama had sewn large seams in her coats which held food. A Belgian woman with a small child seemed safe; at least, that was what I hoped. I was frightened and excited. However, I know that Mama was terrified when we got to the border check sites. A part of me was able to see these trips as adventures and I truly believed that Mama would know what to do to keep us safe. Mama used my patched eye as a reason for our traveling, but I wondered, "What would happen if we get caught?" I don't think Mama even wanted to think about the answer to this question.

On these trips, we were shown around the farm. Opa Huige was so proud when I commented on how clean the barns were. He had many animals and a lot of cattle and their barns were definitely a lot cleaner than the farm in Belgium where we were given refuge. I felt proud that he took my comment to heart and was so pleased that he validated my observations. I did not get to know Papa's family well, as distance proved quite a problem. I had often wished I knew all of these uncles and aunts better and I did get to know many of them during my many visits as an adult.

It seems that during wartime, simple injuries become serious very quickly. I injured my arm climbing a tree and it quickly turned into blood poisoning. As there were no antibiotics, it took many months of painful treatments to heal this wound. Mama had to clean the wound three times a day and during those times, she would tell me to offer my pain up to God. I think I would have preferred not having pain to offer to God. I definitely took a lot of Mama's time and attention. I also had my tonsils out and after leaving the hospital, I started bleeding again and had to be rushed back so the bleeding could be stopped. I had more than my share of physical issues and Corrie says that she often felt jealous of the attention I got. I can really understand that. I think that we, unfortunately, learned that injuries brought scarce and much-needed attention. With all the tension and stress, none of us got what we needed. We did not starve physically, but our emotional needs were not met. Mama did what she could, but with all that was going on in our world, in our lives and with her own unmet needs, it was not enough. No one could have met our young needs.

We were used to the parades of soldiers goose-stepping through the streets. They were usually announced by loud thuds in unison. I could almost feel the ground shake. The soldiers would have their very neat uniforms with many shiny buttons. Their bodies would be tight and straight and they had very grim expressions on their faces.

They all looked so determined that I wondered where they were going and what they were going to do when they got there. They would lift their legs in unison and then their feet would crash on the ground. It was quite a sight. I sometimes wondered why we all rushed outside to see the parade. It felt like we had to be there to watch. I didn't cheer and I didn't really make noise. I just stood there and looked.

One day, I heard on the radio that the Allies had won. I was not sure what that meant, but everyone around me was happy and cheered. I knew it must be something wonderful. Then, people in the neighborhood started yelling, "The Americans are coming."

I knew I was an American and that American soldiers were fighting in the war, but I wondered what this all meant. "Was my Papa coming?" "No," said Mama and she explained that the American soldiers were coming to free us. At least, that is what I understood. She also warned, "Do not take chocolates from the American soldiers." At this point, I was really confused. I wondered what could be wrong with the chocolate. We had not had any chocolate and I wanted some if they would give it to us. In thinking about this as an adult, I believe that Mama was worried about the chaos and possible abuse of little girls by overzealous soldiers who might be using chocolate as a lure. I didn't understand. I just wanted to taste chocolate.

Then, the parade of soldiers began. We could hear the loud, happy music. Our neighbors filled the sidewalks to see what would happen. We were jumping up and down and cheering. We were so excited. It was funny when we saw the soldiers, because the Americans were walking like it was a Sunday walk. They didn't have the same steps as the Germans. They also were not clean and tidy and had no shiny buttons. In fact, they were quite dirty. They were laughing and talking and, to my great delight, they were throwing candy at us. My sisters and I gathered up all of the candy that we could. I was careful not to take the chocolates, but my sisters did take all the chocolate they could. I felt so confused about the chocolate, but my sisters said they loved it and they didn't die from it. The war was apparently over. It was confusing, however, that the bombing continued for several months. It was unclear to me what "over" meant when it came to the war.*

*Wikipedia states that in the six months following Allied liberation, Belgium towns were widely targeted by unpiloted German V-bombs. A total of 2,342 of these rockets (1,610 of the more advanced V-2s and about 732 V-1s) fell in a ten-mile radius of Antwerp alone. V-bombs were responsible for killing 5,000 people and injuring 21,000, mostly in Antwerp and Liege. We experienced this in Lokeren.

PAPA RETURNS

We survived, and around 1947, Papa came home. He was not our handsome savior. He was fat and had lost a lot of his hair. There was less of Mama for us when we again became an intact family. Papa had not been around children for years and was very short-tempered with us when we did what children are prone to do: make noise. This was the mysterious person we had been praying for. Papa said we all had to move to America or that was the end of his marriage to Mama. We didn't talk about moving. We had no choice. Mama was concerned about her parents and their needs. She believed that if she left, she would never see them alive again. She finally agreed to uproot us and take us to the land where *the streets are paved with gold.* I don't think she really believed this, but she did believe that life would be easier and better for us if she agreed to go.

I remember being terribly confused. This man, my Papa, was a stranger to me and not even someone I really liked. He was an angry man; it did not take much for him to lose his temper. I had believed he would be an all-knowing, wonderful, kind person who would make problems melt away. Instead, the tensions were higher than ever. This felt even worse than the war. No matter what we said or did, it seemed to be wrong. He made no effort to get to know us and he didn't seem to care. It was as though the war left the streets but moved into our house.

Mama had us eat separately from her and Papa as we were noisy and made Papa nervous. Mama was worried and torn. She had been given an ultimatum that we all go to another country with this man or Papa would leave us all behind. I did not like this and I did not want to go, but for Mama's sake, I decided I would try to be better and not cause any problems.

My future was decided for me. I would leave everything and everyone familiar to me and head into the unknown. I initially tried to get excited about the move; however, I was totally bereft when I heard that Marieke would not go with us. She was a family member and I wanted to stay with her. That choice was not mine to make. We all packed some of our things and we could take one toy with us. We had to take a small boat to get to the big boat. Marieke went with us to the big boat and Corrie got to sit with her on the small boat. Then we said a very tearful goodbye. I can't believe the intensity of my grief, but it stayed with me for a long time. We took an ocean liner to Newark, New Jersey. As we pulled away from the shore, I asked Mama, *"Will we see Ooma and Oopa again, and what about cousin Ria? Who will look after them?"* Mama looked so sad; tears welled up in her eyes. She didn't speak, but I thought I knew her answer. I turned away from the distant image of the country that was my home and found a seat. I didn't understand the pain in my heart, but I knew I had to think of something else. I needed to move into my new life. I needed to believe that we would be alright and that I must think good thoughts.

Papas Family

Mama's Oma and Opa Qwistwater

Mama and Papa

Mama and Oom mil

First Communions

Mama, Kristy,

Corrie's Class

Mama Corrie.

Playing in our yard

Our first boat going to America

AN OCEAN VOYAGE TO A NEW WORLD

I thought that the ship we were to travel on was huge, but Mama said it was not considered a big boat. It had a number of decks and we were assigned a small room with four berths, that is, beds. There were stairs all over the place and it was fun going up and down when the ship was rolling from side to side. Mama said it was a Liberty ship. I didn't know what that meant, but when I was older, I found out it was one of the ships built quickly during the war, with the expectation that it would probably be sunk before it got to Europe. They were often bombed on their first journey across the Atlantic. The whole family, except for me, was seasick most of the way to the United States. Corrie lost her toy early on in the trip. I wandered all over the boat while the others remained in the cabin. There were a lot of people on this boat and quite a few children. Since I was not sick, I was able to play with the new friends I made.

I had never imagined that there was a sea this large. It seemed like it would never end. At times, the water was so full of huge waves that I couldn't walk on the deck because I could get tossed into the sea. When I was again allowed on the main deck, a big wave hit the boat. Water sprayed all over the deck and got me completely wet. I was frightened yet also strangely excited. I looked at the waves and dreamt about my future. I would make it good. I will leave the war behind. I will find success for myself. Mama always told me that *"no matter what you get into, you will come out of it smelling like roses."* I wasn't sure what she meant, but I liked the picture. I would end up smelling like a rose and all would be OK, no matter what I got into. I stayed on deck and attempted to plan what my life would be. I was not about to go to the cabin and deal with everyone who was sick. I loved staying on deck and staring at the huge ocean ahead of me. With each day, the distance from the home I knew grew greater. Could I make this a good thing…this move…this new life? This was beginning to feel a bit like an adventure. I decided that being afraid all the time was not what I wanted. I would work on seeing the good in this new world. Papa was not with us as he said he needed to leave before we did to prepare a place for us to live.

We were all sad and confused. It seemed like everyone around me was crying. From now on we were to speak English, not Flemish. I was upset about this. I felt sad. So many people on the boat felt the mixture of sadness and excitement I was feeling as we were embarking on this new adventure. I was also secretly excited and imagined what the adventure ahead of us would bring. I had to be secretive about my excitement because Mama and my sisters were sad. We were leaving the war behind us. We were going to a NEW country and maybe we were done with seeing bombed-out houses. I said nothing about this because everyone else seemed so very sad. Mama cried a good deal of the time. She tried to hold her feelings back but it was all too much for her. She was leaving everything and everyone she knew and had no idea what was waiting for her on the other side of this huge ocean. The very powerful woman I knew was nowhere to be seen. She was now the victim of the unfamiliar. She later told me that what she was most worried about was that she did not really know Papa. She hoped she was making the right decision for all of us. She said she really missed her Mama and Papa and her brothers. Ooma and Oopa died within six months of our departure from Belgium. Mama felt guilty and thought they died from broken hearts.

I thought the sea would go on forever. I was ready for my journey to end. When would we see land again? One morning, there was a tidal wave of excitement on the ship with passengers rushing to the upper deck. Everyone was talking loudly and excitedly. I decided to go with them. They were yelling, *"America...America...America,"* and I joined in. Once on the deck, I saw land. Everyone was pointing in the same direction and suddenly, I saw what they were pointing at. It was what Mama had said we would see: Lady Liberty...the Statue of Liberty. I jumped up and down and made all of the happy sounds that I could. I couldn't believe how thrilling this experience was.

"Mama, we made it...we're in America!. Come on deck and see. Everyone is singing and dancing. Come up." Ria, Mama, and Corrie came and joined me in cheering for our new country. It was the first time in a long time that we had laughed together. We made it!

EPILOGUE: THE SISTERS RETURN

My sisters and I returned to Belgium in 1992 for a large gathering of the Huige family from all over the world. Cousin Ria joined us when we visited Antwerp and Lokeren. We had no idea how to locate Marieke, but we were determined to do so. We stopped first at the house which had been our home. The new residents were happy to meet the children they had heard so much about and to show us the changes in the home. It was magnificent and I thought it was larger than I remembered. Corrie thought it was smaller. The entrance hall for the cars was very much the same; however, the naked Venus de Milo had become a clothed Hermes. We laughed at that change. The house was completely updated with elegant fixtures and furniture. It was stunning! The garden, which had been our refuge, was now taken over by a large tennis court and a lovely patio. The vegetable garden and rabbit warren were gone.

After visiting the house, we went to the church. The moment we entered the church, all four of our heads went back and looked at the ceiling and…yes…the stars were still shining as brightly as ever and we all thought, *"All is well with the world."* While there, we met an undertaker and Corrie decided to ask if he knew a coal merchant. She went on to describe Marieke and her husband. He said, *"Oh yes,"* and promptly told us approximately where she lived. Before we knew it, everyone in the town seemed to know that *"the Americans"* were looking for Marieke. We had not even gotten to her home when we saw an old woman riding a bicycle towards us.

It was Marieke. We really felt as though we had come home. She was overjoyed to see us again and we were happy to meet her family.

48

AMERICA

We arrived at the docks in what I thought was New Jersey. All we saw was poverty and a lot of poor people who seemed to be wandering about, unsure of where to go. Just like us. A lot of the people looked like they were dirty and their clothes were torn and old. They didn't look the way I thought Americans should look. I thought that Americans were happy most of the time and that they had all of the food and things they wanted and needed. Dad had said that the streets were "paved with gold." I thought that meant that everyone was rich and since there was no war, everything should look good. The happiness we had known a short time earlier disappeared. Everyone looked miserable. The buildings around us looked like they were about to fall down. Nothing looked like it had been taken care of. We spent a lot of time sitting on our luggage, waiting for something to happen. I had no idea what to expect or what was going on. What were we waiting for? This wasn't what I had been hoping to see. I had no idea what was going on. For the first time in my life, I became aware that people came in different colors. I saw and heard brown and black people yelling at each other in a language I could not understand. I didn't think they were angry, but I was not sure. I felt afraid.

Everything also looked dirty and garbage was everywhere. I think that we were all confused. The world looked so different from what I was used to seeing and from what I had expected to see. Lokeren had been clean. I had been used to Mama washing the street in front of our house, as did our neighbors. Even during a war, we felt the need to be clean. We had been traveling for at least ten days and were all exhausted. Feeling as confused and tired as we were only complicated our distress. No one seemed to have any idea as to what to do, where to go, who could help us. My sisters and I were American citizens, so there was no problem with our paperwork; however, Mama was not a citizen and that apparently took extra time.

After some time, we finally got on a train and headed for Detroit, Michigan. Mama again said that from now on, we were to speak English, not Flemish. This really shut me up as I was used to talking a lot and now, I didn't know the English words I needed in order to express what I wanted to say. Mama knew a few American words and phrases. I was grateful that I could at least ask where the bathroom was. Mama said she would teach us what she knew and that once we had friends and school, we would quickly learn. I wasn't so sure but I wanted to believe her. Life as we knew it was over. World War II, as we had known it, was over for us. Now, we needed to plunge into a world that was completely unknown to us. I was very curious about this new world. I was also frightened.

Would I be able to forge a path for myself? What would happen to me? Could my father give us the love we needed?

I'm in my new world now. I need to think about what I want things to be like. I want Mama back. I want the family I've always known back, but I know that's not possible. I know I won't get the whole of my family back, but maybe we can make a good family that's kind to one another and that enjoys being together. Can I find a way to deal with the father I have, not the one I fantasized about? So far, he's a disappointment and I am afraid of him. I want friends and school. I want life to settle down for me. I WANT PEACE IN MY WORLD AND IN MY HOME. I want to find a place for myself in this world. I really do want a family. I also want to make something of myself, to BE someone.

AMERICAN GIRLS 1947-1951

English…only English…Remember, it is Mom and Dad now. No Flemish for us. It feels like we've lost Mama and Papa. Mom said we would learn our new language quicker if we spoke only English. I don't know if I want her to be right. I know I don't want to give up Flemish.

Life changed when we came ashore in our new country.

Our world is different now. Everything has a different name. It is so much work remembering all of the new words thrown our way each day. Where is the familiar? I have never felt so tired in my whole life. There is no comfortable place to retreat. As I think about those times, I remember my whole body being tangled up in the frustration of not being able to express what I was feeling. I can still feel my body and mind-twisting painfully as I try to explain what I want, need, and am experiencing. I need to think of what I want first in Flemish and then find some words to translate my thoughts into English. In the meantime, I haven't the faintest idea what the people around me are saying. The sentences I manage to come up with are no longer pertinent to where the conversation has moved. I feel lost. Pointing only gets me so far. I feel humiliated because I can't express myself. I feel so stupid and people look at me like I haven't got a brain in my head. My sisters are in the same boat. We cheat and speak Flemish as the three of us are lying in the same bed, trying to get to sleep. It is such a wonderful relief to be understood; we don't care if we get into trouble.

Corrie and I have gotten into the bad habit of tearing the wallpaper from the wall by our bed. This is one way of speaking and asserting ourselves. Ria tends to be quiet. She is never one to speak about her feelings, but it is clear that she, too, is unhappy and feels tortured in trying to express herself. Struggling to find the right word and hearing the laughter when I am wrong is painful. I was used to being the smartest in the group and no one laughed at me. This is a different world. Nothing is familiar. We used to have our garden as a retreat zone. We could relax and play and slowly sort things out. The familiar provided safety and understanding in times of crisis, but even that respite is no longer there. In Belgium, we had familiar faces with familiar expressions that expressed familiar feelings in a familiar language, but this level of understanding is gone. Mom looks sad and bewildered. In Belgium Dad had looked frustrated and angry when relating to us. What will he be like when he is with us now? He always looks jovial when drinking and relating to his friends. No one seems receptive to confused children.

The train trip to Detroit is long and sad. Mama...I mean, Mom...continues to be tearful and anxious. She seems like a different person. I think she is worried about what Dad will do with us and what is facing her in this new world. He had trouble dealing with our play and noise in Belgium; what will he do now? Mom is worried and so I worry. She says she doesn't know what had happened to Dad since we had all lived together before the war. He is different from the person she married. She suggests that we be patient and pray that things will settle down. She further thinks that maybe all of the upheaval in our lives is making things feel worse than they probably are.

During the trip to Detroit, I spend my time looking out of the windows of the train. Everything looks so different from the country we had just left. The houses are really unusual for me. They are not attached to one another and do not seem as tall. In fact, many of the houses look very small and short. There is a lot of beautiful open country with an occasional house. We go through what Mom says are several states, even though we are still in the same country. I can't believe how big America seems to be. Some of the areas we pass are very interesting and everything is quite different from Belgium. Everything seems bigger, except for the small houses. There are some beautiful open areas, but there are also a lot of places that seem sad and very run down. I am surprised at how different this world is proving to be.

Dad picks us up at the Detroit train station. The station itself is absolutely beautiful with marble floors that look like they belong in a castle. I begin to think that maybe living here won't

be so bad. It could be okay. The people around us look busy…but…OK. They don't look angry, but they really look quite different. The men wear suits that look new and they have very shiny shoes. In fact, it is interesting to me that there are people in the station who polish shoes for a living. There is a big chair that a man can sit in and the shoeshine man cleans his shoes. The two people usually say very little to one another but the task is done perfectly. There are also places to get food and many stores where you can buy anything you want. People seem to be rushing from place to place. Everybody looks very dressed up. The ladies have dresses that seemed fancy, high-heeled shoes, and nylons. Real nylons, not the brown, line up the back of their legs like Marieke. Thinking about Marieke makes my stomach hurt and I tear up. I try very hard to think about other things.

We got into a beautiful new green car and Dad said it was ours. Wow…I like that.

"Where is our house?" I asked.

"We don't have a house yet; I need to buy a business first. But don't worry, we're staying with some friends of mine for the time being."

I got worried. That first day, we drove to Jackson, Michigan. It was another very long trip. I got carsick as Dad smoked cigars in the car and between the movement of the car and the smell of the cigar, my body gave up and I threw up all over his beautiful car. So, I managed to make him very angry at me on our first day together.

We spent our first few months with Dad's friends. They were very old and I don't think they understood kids. They were kind but tended to tease me as I had a front tooth missing and Mr. C. kept sticking his finger in my mouth while laughing at me. I hated this; it felt icky to me, but Mom said to be nice and not make a fuss. I could tell she was worried that if I complained, we would be asked to leave. I don't think we had any other place to go. I did not make a fuss. I would have done anything to go to school. I would have done anything to just get out of that house. We hadn't gone anywhere since we got there, and I felt like a prisoner.

We didn't go to school because we were not going to stay in Jackson. Mom spent time with us teaching us some English. We missed our school chums from Belgium and didn't venture outside as everything felt so strange. I think we all worried that we would also lose Mom. She was acting so strange, and didn't resemble the Mama we had grown up with. We were frequently reassured that we would soon be in our own home and then we could go back to school. We couldn't wait to finally have a place we could call our own. I missed everything that felt familiar, even going to church. In Belgium, we were often bored in church, looking up at the stars on the ceiling and whispering to one another. Now, we begged to find a church and looked forward to being bored by a familiar ritual.

Mom said that when we had a home, we would also find a church. She agreed that she also missed our Sundays in church and we felt relief that she felt feelings similar to those we were dealing with.

55

A NEW HOME FOR US

Dad bought a bar, and Mom was not happy. I think she felt ashamed at the idea of running a bar and, even worse, owning the bar. Her family did not drink much and I don't believe they would have approved of her working in a place where people got drunk. The house we were looking forward to living in turned out to be the apartment above the bar. It was filthy and looked like it was as worn out as we were. It smelled terribly from cigarettes, cigars, and beer. The walls were brown from the bar smoke. Mom said we could fix it up and make it our own. I did not want to make it my own. I felt like crying. Everything was a mess. Our suitcases were all over what was to be our room and there was no place to put our limited belongings. I was grateful that my sisters seemed to feel the same way I did.

We sat on the bed and listened to the noise around us. The bar was located in Grosse Pointe Farms, and its name was the Manor Bar. It was located on a major road, Mack Avenue, and we heard a lot of traffic. The sounds coming from the bar itself were very loud and scary. We heard the voices of men yelling and sounding angry. We later understood that a lot of the words they tended to use were profane. This went on until 2 o'clock in the morning and started back up at 7 a.m. Another problem with the bar was that many of the patrons were heavy smokers and the smell of stale smoke touched everything in our upstairs apartment. The house reeked of smoke and we were never able to rid the place of a smell I grew to hate. I believed my body smelled of this smoke, my clothes smelled, and I was sure that the friends I might be able to make at school would be repelled by the odor. Even worse was the fact that I felt ashamed to live above this bar. There was no way that I would ask a friend to come and play at my home. I didn't even believe that if I had a friend that her parents would allow her to play with me or visit my home.

It was late spring and there were only a few more weeks of school. Ria and I started in the Catholic school just a couple of miles from home, while Corrie went to a public school named Kerby as there was no room at the Catholic school. Corrie had to take a school bus to her school and she managed to do so in the mornings; however, at the end of the day, she had no idea what to do, so she just stayed at school. The school called the police and she got a ride home in a police car. Corrie found this exciting as the policeman put the siren on and she waved to people who looked at her in her chariot. What a great trip home. This went on for several days and on the fourth day, the chief of police took her home and spoke to Mom and Dad about their errant child.

"I think she is enjoying this way too much. We've tried to explain to her that she needs to take the bus, but she doesn't seem to grasp what we are saying. She's a great kid but we can't continue to give her chauffeur service. Please let her know what she needs to do to get home," said the chief.

The chief later became a good friend of my father's and Corrie took the school bus. Her exciting adventures were over at this point. I do have to admit that we had a good laugh over Corrie's school adventures.

One thing I had a great deal of trouble dealing with was an almost universal greeting: "Oh, you must be so glad to be in the United States! You are so very lucky." I did not feel glad or lucky. I had left most of the people I loved in Europe. I had left my Ooma, my Oopa, Marieke, my uncles and aunts and cousins. I left my school and the friends I loved and my very beautiful house. I even left my language. My mother, who used to be happy and fun, was now sad most of the time. I was sad most of the time. I lived in a smelly, very dirty, small apartment above a bar, nothing like the house and garden I left. I saw very little of my mom as she now worked in a bar and I was ashamed. Everything and everyone I loved were no longer part of my life. Even my language was gone. And I was supposed to feel happy and lucky? I felt so very angry. I was not allowed to express my feelings. At first, I said nothing to those people who thought I should be so lucky.

Mom said I should simply say, "Oh yes, we are lucky to be here. Thank you."

I felt like throwing up whenever I said these words. Mom was afraid that people would be upset with us if we were not grateful for our new lives. I didn't care if they were upset; I didn't want to say things I did not feel. However, more and more, I repeated these untruths. I felt like such a liar. I wondered how many people were speaking untruths such as mine. How authentic or truthful were people really? Could I believe what people were saying to me? I missed my European family and friends. I missed my language and I missed my mother's wonderful lilac smell. I missed her smile and laugh. Even though there had been a war going on, we had closeness and wonderful family experiences. Nothing could change these thoughts in my mind.

During that first summer in the United States, we took a vacation trip to Petoskey. I thought it was mainly for us to have some fun in the woods. We stayed in a log cabin on a lake. While there, we had a very strange meeting with a woman about Mom's age. Dad was with us, and he was telling this woman that their relationship was over. He had apparently had an affair with her throughout the war and Mom said he needed to "finish" with it, whatever that meant.

Dad said he was sorry to both Mom and this woman. I only heard him apologize a couple of times after this experience. I never did understand why we had to be there to hear this apology. I felt like crawling away and finding a way not to be present. I felt very uncomfortable. This did explain, though, why he didn't come to us right after the war and why we had not heard from him for years. It probably also explained why Dad was so unhappy with us. I often wondered why he came back to us in Belgium, as he didn't seem very happy with us. We also were not happy with him.

After this uncomfortable scene, we managed to have a good time at the cabin. Later in the week, we found a very unusual playmate. I don't quite remember if he was a relative of Johnnie's or simply someone we met at a friend's house in Petoskey. Father Solanus was a Capuchin monk and he was visiting some of his family or friends. I have no idea why we were at this house, but it felt like a wonderful, safe, and quiet space. He was very old with a lot of wrinkles but very happy eyes. I think we played some board games and talked a lot. He loved to play. We spent most of the day in this beautiful backyard which reminded me of our yard in Lokeren. He was a lot of fun to play with. He was probably the most serene person I have ever met. I felt at ease with him immediately and at one point, when my hand touched his, I felt an incredible sense of peace I had not felt for a long time. I felt happy. He was a good person. I felt in my heart that there was something very special about him, and apparently, I was correct. Other people had the same experience with him. In 2018, the Catholic Church gave him the title of "Blessed," and he was later declared a saint. I found out he worked at a food kitchen for the poor in his church for his entire life, the Capuchin Soup Kitchen. He was a very old man when he spent part of a day with us, but he had a wonderful child just under his skin. I only spent a short time with this peaceful person, but the happiness

I felt that day was unlike anything I felt before or since, and seemed to bring some sense of lightness into my world. I felt so serene. I prayed that I could come to peace with the many changes in my life. I wish I could remember more of this experience. Mom and our family continued to contribute to the Capuchin Soup Kitchen for years. I was an adult before I connected this donation with the little monk we met as children.

In September, all three of us went to Catholic school. Corrie and I were put in the same classroom. I was so insulted. I was physically much bigger than these first-graders and my mind was operating in a different world. Here I was, stuffed into a small desk and treated like a first-grader. I was so embarrassed, I turned red and I felt like crying. I did cry.

"I don't want to be here. I feel dumb being with the little kids."

The principal must have seen my discomfort and she kindly told me: "As soon as your English improves and we see that you can handle your other classes in English, we will move you to the next grade. We really want you to succeed."

I understood what she was saying and agreed with the plan. I worked very hard at all of my subjects and was quite successful. I ended this year in the third grade and moved into fourth grade. I felt as though I had won a prize.

I could deal with teasing with respect to my language skills, but I had a really hard time being in a class with much smaller and younger children. While we were in the same classroom, I could tell that Corrie was having a hard time. She felt very insecure and because of her fears, she would constantly talk to me in Flemish. The teacher became so irritated that, at one point, she taped Corrie's mouth shut. I was horrified. I could not believe what was happening.

This world did not feel safe. The other kids in the room laughed, but I remained quiet. I always felt some guilt about doing nothing to help, knowing all the while that I loved whispering in Flemish and perhaps instigated Corrie to talk. I didn't tell the teacher that I thought Corrie was afraid and I felt guilt that I didn't complain about her punishment. I felt I let Corrie down. I was not there for her when it counted. Corrie and I did not tell Mom about this teacher. We were both embarrassed and were worried that Mom would be angry with us for our behavior. We also knew Mom was dealing with so many problems and we didn't want to make things worse for her. We spoke to one another about this experience, and decided we would need to be much more careful when it came to school.

While at this school, I spent a good deal of time daydreaming. It is amazing how difficult it is to operate in a language that feels so totally foreign. The only people in my world who had familiar smells, speech, and mannerisms were Mom and my sisters. I was grateful that they were in my life. I believe that Mom tended to discount the significance of having a native language to go home to. The familiar words and sounds of your early language provide a safe world and they make stresses easier to manage. All three of us really missed these familiar sounds.

There was a church connected to the school, and we attended every Sunday. This was also a place where I felt grounded as the ritual, with its smells and bells, was the same as the mass in Belgium. It was the only place where the language was the same in America as it was in Belgium: **LATIN**. We didn't understand much of it in either country, but neither did the other people in church. The sounds and music, however, were familiar. It was a peaceful place to be. We did not need to understand the language as the tones and sounds were familiar to us. Corrie and I made our first communions at St. Clare's church. While it was a beautiful and meaningful event, I was again reminded that I was behind my age group. I was again the biggest person in the group.

In America 1948

62

Family 1950

Johnny's wedding

It was hard getting used to having Mom busy in the bar and not available to us. She was so tired, but she always had a good dinner on the table. It was sad, however, that we did not eat together as a family most of the time. Mom and Dad were usually in the bar at dinner time. Johnnie came to stay with us and he also worked in the bar. I didn't know him. He was grown up now and he even had a girlfriend. He had the front bedroom and the three of us girls were still needing to share a room and a bed. It was crowded, and we were all on edge and quite ready to either burst into tears or get angry. Our new way of life was so different from what we had left behind in Europe.

One day, I needed to tell Mom something and I had to go into the bar because it was important. I crept down the stairs and I hoped to make a quiet, quick entrance and exit. I had never been in a bar before. I was terrified as I cautiously opened the door and winced when it creaked loudly. I saw Mom sitting at a table with a beer and a cigarette, talking to customers. Everyone looked my way as the door howled on opening. I was shocked when I saw Mom and immediately felt furious. I had never seen her with a cigarette and a beer. I screamed and babbled on in Flemish. I cried and cried…

"I can't believe you are doing this. Smoking and drinking. You're like a fallen woman. Ooma would be so mad." I ripped the cigarette from her mouth and stomped on it, yelling and crying. "How could you do this? I'm ashamed of you! I can't believe that you are doing this! We've lost you!" I was sobbing and shaking as I yelled.

Mom was shocked and took me upstairs to help me calm down. I was frightened that she would be angry and yell at me, but she wasn't angry. She wasn't even angry that I had yelled in Flemish. She was kind and understood my reaction. Actually, she seemed more sad.

"I know this is all very hard for you. I am still the same person. I'll promise you that I won't start smoking and that I will never be drunk. I'm sorry that I shocked you and I know you don't see me as the same person I was in Belgium, but I am the same person. I know that life is difficult for you now. It is for me also, but I will always be here when you need me. Don't be afraid to get upset with me. Life will get easier."

I accepted this, but still decided that this was proof that my Mama was really gone. I believed that Mom also did some thinking and decided not to smoke. I didn't see her smoke again until I was in my twenties. She did have an occasional drink but reassured me that she would not get drunk. I believed her and I never saw her drunk. This whole experience solidified for me that bars were terrible places and that they destroyed people, even people who had been wonderful before exposure to a bar. Mom was no longer on a pedestal for me. I hated bars more than ever. I was ashamed of where I lived, and I was ashamed of both my mother, and my father.

My sisters and I had always been incredibly close, but now I could feel us drifting away from one another. It is disconcerting when you have always relied on sisters to be there and suddenly, they have lives outside of home. Ria, maintaining consistency, buried herself in her books. It was like Ria had just decided to not be there, to just disappear. Corrie made friends very quickly and enjoyed going out to play whenever she could. She even got up the nerve to climb to the top of a tree in the empty lot next door. Once at the top, she turned to cheer for herself and promptly fell to the ground.

"Hey…look at me! I'm up with the birds. Oh, my goodness…help…I'm falling."

Her friends on the ground gasped with fear and ran to her. Someone hurried to get Mom; however, Mom surprised us all with her anger. "What on earth were you doing up in that tree? That is not ladylike behavior and it better not happen again! Come here and let me see what damage was done."

Thank goodness Corrie suffered only a few scrapes and bruises. She was loudly told not to try anything so wild and dangerous again. I'm sure that message stayed with her for a few minutes, as she remained ready to try anything new and exciting.

I withdrew to books and also wandered the neighborhood, exploring everything I could check out. Some of that exploring proved to be dangerous. There was a gas station that also repaired cars and sold candy on Mack Avenue but on the opposite corner of the bar. I was about nine years old and thought I could buy some candy at the gas station when the mechanic engaged me in conversation. He seemed like a nice person and I felt very much alone. One day, he started touching me in ways I instinctively knew were wrong. I think he only touched my shoulder, but his touch and the way he looked terrified me.

"Stop, don't touch me. Get away from me. I don't like what you are doing."

I yelled for him to stop and kicked him. I ran like my life depended on it. I managed to get away, but I was terribly shaken and felt I had done something terribly wrong. I thought it must be my fault that this man tried to touch me. What had I done? I should not do it again, whatever it might be. I was afraid. I had no idea what to do. I don't remember telling anyone what happened, but from then on, I stayed very close to home, my trust shaken. I wanted to warn Ria and Corrie, but my shame kept me from disclosing what had happened. I also felt shame, believing that I must have done something to cause this man to hurt me. I felt guilty about not warning my sisters, but I found out later that Mom warned them not to go to that station for anything. I really missed the safety of Belgium. I wondered why Mom didn't talk to me about this man; I thought she must have known something about what happened. Maybe she was angry with me for going there. I wished we could talk.

In spite of worries, we did have a lot of fun, especially Corrie and me. On Saturdays, we would walk the mile or so to the Woods Theater, where we proceeded to work our way into free tickets. Mom knew nothing about this, and I'm sure she would have been angry, but we still were game to try our deception. We decided that this was a time when speaking Flemish could work. We pretended we knew very little English and didn't understand money. We were aiming for sympathy. We knew they would sometimes appoint kids like us as greeters. .(I'm not sure what the role was) They would give us cowgirl hats and we would say hello to people, hand out gifts, show people to their seats, and tell people where the bathrooms were. If we were greeters, we got in free. Somehow or other, we managed to get these free tickets quite often. We had more fun around that theater and sometimes stayed for the second feature. This was quite late for children our age and it was often dark when we were walking back home. Mom was usually busy in the bar and didn't realize we weren't home, so we got away with this mischief.

Corrie and I also tried to work our magic on the buses. We tried saying we were Siamese twins and should only pay one fare. We did get away with this at least once, leaving the bus driver doubled over with laughter. We felt pride in our victory. Ria went to the movies with us a few times, but she complained, "I'm ashamed to be seen with you guys because you get so nuts at times. Why don't you act more normal?"

I concluded that the older you get, the more apt you are to feel ashamed and have to behave properly, missing the fun.

We had some fun, but on the whole, things were not going well for me. I was plagued with anxiety and frequently sick. My stomach hurt constantly, and the doctor said he could find nothing wrong. I had frequent headaches, got many colds and fevers, and had difficulty falling and staying asleep. Nightmares took over my nights. I chose not to spend nights at friend's homes because I didn't want to scare them with my screams. Mom said I would outgrow the nightmares, but I did not. I was terrified at night and would often take my blanket and sit outside the door of Mom and Dad's bedroom just to feel a bit closer to what I believed was safety. I jumped at the slightest noise and often cried for no reason at all. I finally decided to pretend that everything was good. I became quite adept at this pretense. I just did not talk about what was happening with me.

Life above the bar meant quiet time for us and noisy time for customers. We had to be quiet and the customers got to make the noise. Mom and Dad worked very long hours, and the longer they owned the bar, the more my father consumed alcohol. He was drunk most days and since he was a diabetic, his blood sugar became very seriously elevated. We knew that things were not good, so we remained fairly quiet, and tried to be good.

We enjoyed Sundays when Mom fixed a very large pot of soup. We kids could eat when we wanted and listen to our favorite programs on the radio. We loved "The Creaking Door," "The Shadow Knows," and other great programs. The three of us really loved being together again. We pulled the shades and drapes and got the room to feel spooky so we could get in the mood. We even stole a few opportunities to sneak in some Flemish. Sometimes, Mom was able to join us. We missed her when she had to work.

We had a way of letting Mom know if we needed her. We had a baseball bat that we banged on the floor by the stairway. One day, the bat fell down the stairs with an incredible clatter. Moments later, it seemed like everyone from the bar was charging up the stairs to see if we were okay. People were laughing when they found out what had happened and we were not in trouble. What a relief! I hate to admit it but I also felt safer and less alone, knowing that there were a lot of people who would help if we needed it. Even though I still did not like the customers at the bar, they seemed less scary or strange and I could see them in a better light.

At this point, we were not living with an active war with clearly defined sides, but we were dealing with a war featuring alcohol as the enemy. Sometimes, when Dad was drunk, he was funny and almost nice. However, most of the time, he got violent at the slightest provocation. We had to learn to step very carefully, to guard our speech, and to watch our facial expressions.

Once, while we were still in the early stages of learning English, Dad tried to do a fatherly activity and took us to the library to get library cards and books. One of the questions we were asked was what my father did for a living. I, of course, always had a ready answer to what was asked.

I piped up, "He eats, sleeps, and drinks!"

I meant to describe his behavior as I felt embarrassed to say that he owned a bar. (I never thought about the possibility of keeping my mouth shut.) I thought that describing what he did would work. It worked for the librarian, but not for Dad. We went home and he went to the bar and drank. In the middle of the night, when he was thoroughly drunk, he staggered upstairs and charged into our room and started to beat us. We all woke up startled and screaming:

"Dad…please don't hurt me…I'm sorry…I'm sorry…You're hurting me!" We managed to roll away from him as far as we could. We were all screaming. " Mom…HELP…HELP…Dad's beating us…please HELP!"

We were all leaping from the bed, holding our pillows for protection. The bed trapped us, and kept us in the room. Sleepy and terrified, we all feared that this giant of a person wanted to kill us. Dad's face was beet red, his eyes were huge and looked like they could pop out of his head. His eyebrows were thick and high and added to his terrifying look. I was the one he was really after, but we were all getting pummeled. We were very grateful that Mom came into the room, grabbed him, and made him stop and go to bed. I was shocked that Mom was as strong as she was. She swept into the room like a superhero and completely took over. Once she got Dad into bed, she came back to us and asked if we were okay. She told us, "It's just the alcohol causing Dad's behavior." I wasn't so sure.

We were shaken by this and realized we had to be much more aware of our words and actions. We had to be careful. Especially around Dad. Spontaneous remarks would not work in this family. The next morning, Dad had forgotten all about the altercation but I did not forget. His violent outbursts continued as his drinking got worse. Mom was more and more exhausted, but she had made her pledge to him and would stand by him.

Mom's depression deepened. Within a year of our arriving in the United States, she heard that Ooma and Oopa died. She loved them deeply and she felt remorse that she was not able to be with them and support her brothers at the time of their parents' deaths. She felt guilty about leaving and believed that they had both died from broken hearts. I also believed this. They had been very attached to us as we were to them. We had lived together during difficult times and had shared our lives. We had been there to love and support one another. Mom's brothers and their families were present for her parents but she mourned them and her inability to be there for them.

"They died because we left. I knew they would not be able to handle losing us. I'll never see them or the family again." We all cried but never talked about them again.

Mom felt guilty about leaving and regretted that, at the moment, we were not happy in the United States. She knew life was not good for us and felt guilt. We all worried that she would also die. I think that all of us, at some time or other, wanted her to tell us that she would die AFTER we did. I wanted to know that I would never have to deal with the world without her. The thought of being left without Mom was terrifying to me. I longed to hear her raucous laugh and see her smiling eyes. She was a different person from the Mama I knew in Belgium. Seeing the change in Mom made me fearful. At this point, I believe that I did not let myself know that Mom had also lived through a lot of trauma, and that she was probably experiencing many of the same symptoms I was living with. I still had to see her as a supermom.

We spent four very hot summers above that bar, with the temperatures well above 100 degrees F. Air conditioning was not available and there were few windows and no cross ventilation. It was so uncomfortable that sleep was impossible and life upstairs in the daytime just didn't work. We had the option of going to the Grosse Pointe Farms Park and swimming in the lake or just sitting outside on the cement in front of our garage reading a book. The park generally won and it was a wonderful place to be. We had never been to a beach park before and hadn't ever gone swimming so this was a great experience. Corrie was lucky that Johnnie took the time to come out and teach her how to swim. Ria and I got no instructions, but we watched and learned on our own. No one, however, had told us about sunburn and as we were three very light-skinned children, we burned and I mean burned. I was the fairest of the three and had blisters all over. Corrie and I actually had to stay in bed for several days to heal. We learned to use sunscreen and seek out shady areas under trees. The park did provide a wonderful place to relax and play. It was a respite. So, on those very hot summer days, we hopped on our bicycles and enjoyed the freedom of the lake.

One of the problems for Mom was that she did not know how to drive. In Europe, she had never needed a car. She had trains and other methods of transport and also her feet. We walked all over the place and if we had to go a long way, we took a train or a tram. In America, she had to rely on Dad to drive her on errands or she could take the bus. The bus was time-consuming and often did not get her where she wanted to be. Dad insisted that Mom learn how to drive. He took her out "driving," at least that is what he called it. He was probably the very worst driving instructor on record as he was very short tempered, impatient with everything Mom did, and he screamed out his orders. He got furious every time Mom froze at his directions. To make matters worse, Dad insisted that we all pile into the back of the car and witness Mom's lessons. Perhaps we also had to witness Mom's inadequacy.

"Get on Mack Avenue… move it!"

Mom, terrified, got onto Mack Avenue and very, very slowly started moving. Other drivers honked and honked as she went slower and slower. As she heard the honking around her, Mom got more and more nervous. Dad, however, got more and more irritated and repeatedly shouted for her to quickly get into the left lane.

"Move it, get into the left lane…what is the matter with you?" he screamed.

Mom's face froze; her eyes had a crazy, angry look and with a jerk, she floored it. The car went airborne into the center island, where it stopped. Shaken, Mom got out of the car and loudly suggested Dad take over. Furiously, she threw him the keys.

"It's all yours, I'm done." She refused to return to the car and walked home.

She was talked into trying to drive two more times. She managed to get into an accident both times and promptly gave up the endeavor. We suggested she get a REAL driving instructor, but she refused. She never drove. This really proved problematic as some places had no public transportation. Not driving worked in Europe as most people just used public transport and there was lots of it, but being a non-driver did not work in America. She was used to going everywhere she wanted without a car, but now she was trapped. Not driving actually kept her confined to the house and made her totally reliant on limited public transportation or someone else to take her where she wanted or needed to go. It also kept her tied to Dad. I often wondered if she would have stayed with Dad if she had felt freer to get from place to place. She was used to being independent in many ways, and this was not the country for independence of movement. Dad was not the partner to encourage independence when it came to Mom's behavior or even her manner of thinking.

Dad loved buying new cars. I don't know where he got the money, but I guess cars were not as expensive then. He would get at least one new car every year. Sometimes, we needed one as he had his share of accidents, but sometimes, it was just to get a shiny new car. As I got older, I have to admit that some of this car stuff rubbed off on me. I loved cars. In Belgium, we always worried about money and I know that Mama was very careful when it came to buying things. We even worried about having enough money for food. Here, Dad bought new cars as though they were free. I didn't understand.

The Huige's had many issues when it came to spending. When you bought something new, you had to say, "Oh, that old thing, I've had it forever; I'm just now deciding to do something with it." Then, we would make up a story where we would try to convince whoever was there that we had worn the item before and that they had seen it. It just hadn't registered with them.

We did this kind of thing from the time we moved to the United States through our teen years and, for some of us, probably adulthood. Mom had a hard time bringing new things into our house. I didn't know if she was afraid of Dad, but this behavior was new for her. She had never been this way in Belgium, although we bought very little during the war. In the United States, she enjoyed shopping and we had fun with her, but the conflict came when it was time to go home and bring the new item into the house. We would sneak around and see if the coast was clear:

"Dad's not here. Hurry."

Then, we would quickly put the bag into our closet and close the door. It's like we all felt incredibly guilty…as though we had committed a crime and were waiting to get reprimanded. Then came the task of bringing the item out of hiding and finding a way to integrate it into our own possessions. We never had these issues in Belgium.

I did not like this change in Mom; she had never been afraid when it came to going to the store. I did not understand why, all of a sudden, we all seemed afraid to spend money and bring our purchases into the house. Why did we have to hide our purchases? Dad could see that we went shopping. Why couldn't we be seen bringing things home from the shopping trip?

As a child, I was a saver. The family laughed and teased me about how hard it was to separate me from my money. I saved every penny I earned from the time we came to America.

"You're a tightwad," Ria would say when I wouldn't give her any money.

I was ten years old and had saved every cent to buy a bicycle for myself. I knew what kind of bike I wanted: a bright red Schwinn. I saved and shopped around for a long time…at least a year. I finally had enough to buy just what I wanted. I was thrilled.

"I'm going to get that shiny red Schwinn bicycle. Tomorrow I will go and buy it. I finally have enough money."

I proudly showed my cash to Mom and Dad; however, the day I planned to make the purchase, Dad took my money and bought me a bike. It was not what I wanted. It was not bright red or even any shade of red; it was not a Schwinn. I was furious and when I expressed my anger, Dad ferociously screamed:

"You are an ungrateful child. Look at what I did for you." I did not respond. I wanted to say that **I** was going to buy **MY** bike. I tried to tell him that this was not the bike I wanted and that I knew exactly what I wanted. He did not listen.

At that point, I decided, "If I save money, I will do so secretly, but better yet, I will spend it while it is still mine." This early decision, felt passionately, has stayed with me. I am apt to buy impetuously before someone takes my funds away.

I kept myself busy with a variety of activities. I loved to sew, knit, crochet, and paint pictures. I was pretty decent at keeping my head in a book and I loved to write, both fiction and poetry.

There was a large field near the bar, and the neighborhood kids played there. We joined in and had a good time playing hide-and-seek and other games. In the summer we would leave the house around 8 a.m. and get home just before dark. When we were not at the park, what we actually did during this time escapes me, but I do know we were tired when we got to our bed. On one foray out of the house, I saw a Kodak Brownie camera in someone's garbage can. I took it and cleaned it up and even got film. It worked. What a find! It was not a terrific camera, but it was a camera. I spent some of my time learning about photography and taking pictures. I had found something I really enjoyed doing. I enjoyed examining my world and composing pictures. I was seldom without this camera and loved looking at the world through the Brownie's lens. I learned to pay attention to details that I had never seen before. Looking through a lens also provided the distance I craved. If I was the photographer, I didn't need to worry about being in the picture. I thoroughly disliked having my picture taken. Cameras and photography have remained important hobbies throughout my life. As an adult, however, I have regretted not having many pictures of myself at various ages.

I was eleven years old and we were just getting used to our home and our school when we got the news that we were moving again. Apparently, Mom and Dad decided that Dad's drinking was out of control and we needed to get out of the bar. I think we were all glad to leave the apartment as none of us were happy to be there. I was not the only one who felt ashamed about living above a bar. We would not miss the bar. We were shocked, however, to learn that we were moving to Canada. Without consulting anyone, not even Mom, Dad had apparently bought a fishing and hunting resort on the Canadian side of Lake St. Clair. None of us, including my Dad, knew anything about resorts, fishing, hunting, or how to run a place like this. The only boat we had ever been on was an ocean liner, and we had no idea what to do with fishing poles. None of us could shoot a gun or even wanted to shoot a gun. We were puzzled about this move, and wondered what we would have to deal with now. We would once more be plunged into a totally new world. It felt like we were once more starting all over. I wondered if my life would be a series of just getting settled and then starting over. I had to accept that I had no choice when it came to where I would live. I would have to make the best of it.

ANOTHER LIFE, ANOTHER COUNTRY

We had been driving for what felt like forever. As usual, I felt carsick, but I didn't throw up. It took hours to cross the border into Canada. There were papers and more papers. Another move. It was hard to believe that we were going to another country. We were all blindsided. "Moving to Canada? Leaving our school? Leaving our friends? What is a resort? Where will we live? Why are we moving?" Mom only told us that Dad was sick and he couldn't continue to work in the bar. We knew he drank too much but we didn't understand that he was "sick." All of our fears returned in full force. We cried: "We don't want to go! Do we have to move again?"

We had no choice and no power. It was hard to convince myself that this was another adventure, but I tried to do so. I was, however, looking forward to no cigarette or cigar smoke and…hopefully, no drinking or at least no getting drunk.

I had no idea where we were going. All that I knew was that we were moving to Canada. It was a long, long drive. All that we saw on the way seemed to be farms and more farms. There were many open fields, some with crops and some growing wild. Where were the towns and libraries and schools and movie theaters? I had only lived in cities and I knew how to get around in places that had public transportation. I saw very little that was familiar. Finally, Dad turned down a small country road. There was one nice farm with a lot of barns and a big house and many cattle. As we continued down the road, the houses became smaller. Some were falling apart with missing windows and failing roofs. "Where are we going? Is our new home down this road?" A creek ran alongside the road. I saw several people who seemed to be working hard digging up gardens and one man was trying to fix his broken porch. My heart sank when I thought…" What does this foretell about where we might live?" Things did not look good.

Finally, we reached a bridge which went over the creek and led to a drive into an area that looked a little bit better than the houses we had passed. Dad said, "This is home." I was surprised, since this place seemed like it was in the middle of nowhere. There were no buses, no stores, no offices, no movie theaters, and no schools. All I saw were some small cabins, a large yard, and many boats. I was disappointed.

As we asked questions about this place, we managed to get some kind of picture of what we would be dealing with. The customers, usually middle-class professional people, came mainly from the United States, and generally came for a week or more. They would rent one of our cabins and a boat. Apparently, it would be a vacation for them. People came to the camp to fish or hunt. They fished for smaller fish such as bluegill, sunfish, or perch. They also hoped to catch very big fish, such as pike, pickerel, and even muskies. When they would hunt in the fall of the year, they often went for ducks such as mallards.

One thing we were not told was that we would be the cleaning crew for the boats and the cabins and we would also be the crew who would rent the boats at all hours of the day and night. On top of that, we were also loaned out to customers as fish cleaners. We had to learn how to remove the scales, open the fish, and take the guts out. Ugh! Talk about a change of lifestyle! I could never have imagined a bigger change in where or how we lived. I was not ready for a big change such as this one.

We drove into the camp area and saw a very large man standing in the yard. This was Jake, a fishing guide and handyman who apparently worked for the camp. He seemed huge to me as he was much taller than Dad and had enormous hands. He was carrying a bucket which had something jumping up and down and slapping the surface of the water.

"Jake will teach you how to clean the boats and fish," Dad said as we were exiting the car.

"Now?…But we just got here!"

"Hey, Frida, come here…I need to teach you something." Jake was yelling at me. He had a strange smile on his face. I was worried…I didn't really know him yet.

"Go with him," Dad said.

I didn't want to go. "Can't Corrie or Ria go? I don't want to go alone."

Dad yelled at me, "You're going, stop complaining."

I walked over to Jake and he motioned that I needed to follow him. We went to what he called the "back bay." It was an area by the water and there was a wooden structure that was angled toward the water. Jake put the pail he was carrying on the ground and pulled out a fish…a big fish.

"There's no time like the present to learn how to clean fish. Are you ready?"

"No!" I yelled.

"Well, better get ready. The first thing you need to do is kill the fish if it's still alive. The best way to do that is to cut its head off."

"Oh…God…you have to be kidding. Ug…this is awful." Jake was handing me a knife AND the fish. I felt like throwing up. I was angry, scared, and totally repulsed.

Jake put the knife in my hand and then put his hand over mine and we cut the head off of the flopping fish. I'd never killed a living thing before, except for mosquitoes or flies. I was shocked.

"Now we have to scale the fish," said Jake, as we traded the knife for a scaler and we" continued to take the scales off the now headless fish. I could see the eyes of the dead fish look at me in a condemning fashion. It was hard for me to look at what we were doing.

"Now," said Jake, "we need to open this critter up and take out the guts."

"You have got to be kidding…ew…I can see them."

Jake once more took my hand and we again switched out the scaler for the knife. We swiftly cut open the belly of the fish and "Oh my God…yuck." The fish's innards popped onto the wooden cutting board. They were slimy and various colors and disgusting.

Jake said, "Oh look…it even has eggs."

"You mean we even killed its babies?" I squealed.

Jake just looked at me, incredulous…"You are really a city girl."

I felt in shock as Jake showed me how to clean the area and the rest of the fish. I couldn't believe I was now living in an area where I would be expected to kill these living things. This new life was definitely different from what I was used to and so far, I did not like it.

I tried to shift my focus. It was not easy, given what I had just experienced. I reminded myself that we were out of the bar. I had previously thought, "Wow, maybe we won't have to deal with drunks." I wasn't sure whether I preferred drunks to dead fish, but it was definitely a different world. I was hopeful about this place, but soon learned that people on vacation often drink to excess and we now had to clean up the messes they left in the cabins. To my distress, Dad often joined in the drinking. I had not escaped alcohol. I now had to deal with both drunks and dead fish.

Our new home was at the end of a very long country road on a small peninsula into Lake St. Clair. The resort consisted of eight cabins, three large guide boats, and forty rowboats that were each 18 feet in length. We were fifty minutes from reasonable-sized towns such as Chatham or Wallaceburg. Our home was a cottage type house with one bedroom and one bath and a good-sized back porch. The house was much smaller than the apartment we had just left. The lake and the surrounding marshes were beautiful, but this way of life was so different from what I was familiar with that I was absolutely stunned as I looked around. The cottages were white with green shutters and each had two bedrooms, a bath, and a kitchen. There was a large bath house with showers and toilets. The resort stood on about ten acres of treed lawn with a large parking area.

"It's really pretty; maybe it won't be so bad. I really like the lake and the marshes and all of the different varieties of birds. There are also lots of small animals running all over the place. It could be interesting."

When I repeated "Maybe it won't be so bad" out loud to myself, I could hear the fear in my voice as I continued…, "It would be great for a week, but to live here all year round does not appeal to me."

However, it soon became very clear that the main workers of this place were my sisters and me. The only other worker I saw was Jake, the handyman I had met earlier that day. He was a bit overwhelming. He was a guide for one of the large inboard motor craft, and described himself as an occasional cleaning person, handyman, and teacher of disgusting things such as cleaning fish. Jake also taught us, Corrie and me, how to clean the rowboats and what an experience that was to remember.

The row boats were made of steel, 18 feet long, and very, very heavy. I had seen people rowing boats, but I had never been in a rowboat and had no idea how to move it from place to place. Jake first showed us how to get into a boat and then how to row a boat. It looked so easy as this lumberjack of a person gracefully hopped into the nearest boat. My turn wasn't nearly as smooth, but I landed on the floor of the boat and quickly found the seat. I couldn't believe how bouncy the boat was on the water. I tried to stand up but I couldn't. I was so grateful I didn't fall in the water as I was not a very good swimmer. I found the oars, and was surprised by how heavy they were.

"Put the oars in the oarlock," shouted Jake

"Where are the oarlocks?

Exasperated, Jake showed us what he wanted us to do.

Now, to put them in the oar locks as Jake instructed. It was really funny seeing Corrie and me going around in circles as we tried to go straight.

"How do you make this thing go straight?" I asked.

Jake shouted orders at us, but I was so engrossed in trying to make the boat go where I wanted that I barely heard him.

"Stop what you're doing and pay attention to me," he yelled. "If you want to go straight, you need to apply the same pressure to both oars."

I had no idea that you needed to put the same amount of pressure on each oar to go straight, but first, we had to be pointed in the right direction. This lesson seemed to go on forever and I was so tired I was ready to quit. I was wet from the water and from sweat and red from the heat, but somehow, I managed to go in a straight line.

"Why do we have to know how to row?" I asked.

"That's a stupid question. You just have to know how to row! You have a resort. Your business is boats…and you have to get the boats over to the hoist and pulley over there to clean them." Jake looked exasperated and pointed to an elaborate pulley system. I had no idea how this was to work.

"The boat needs to go in between these ropes," said Jake, now frustrated with his recalcitrant students. "Once you have the boat here, you need to get out of the boat." After a good deal of trial and error, I finally got to the pulley.

I struggled to get myself up and out of the boat. The shore seemed a lot higher up than the boat, but I did finally crawl up onto the land. I was exhausted and hotter than I can ever remember being.

"Now," said Jake, "you have to pull on these ropes.

I pulled and pulled, but I'd never tried to lift anything this heavy. My hands and arms hurt. Finally, I managed to lift the boat on its side, but "What do I do now?" I said, struggling as I held onto the rope. I could tell I couldn't let go or I'd have to start over and I wasn't ready to do that.

"You have to tie the rope here to keep the boat from falling back into the water." Jake was pointing to a steel hook-like thing on a nearby tree. He helped me wrap the rope around the hook. Finally, I could let go. I rubbed my hands, hoping the pain would go away.

"You're not done yet. Now you have to clean the boat. You need to brush it out with a broom and then wash it using the hose."

I was terrified as I had to lean over the water to do this. I was afraid I would fall in. Three years later, I did fall in and almost cut my big toes off on both of my feet. I needed a lot of stitches. Dad got so angry at me that the customers had to take me to the hospital. That first day, I knew this was a dangerous task and I didn't want to get hurt. I was very careful. The boat was really yucky inside, and I brushed and brushed and then sprayed with water that got both the boat and me soaked. I did learn how to do this task as did Corrie.

After this initial introduction to boat cleaning, my hands and my whole body hurt from this trial run. I did not know if I could do this again. I knew, however, that I would not have a choice in this matter. I would have to learn how to do this job no matter how difficult it was for me. I didn't want to do this chore, but I didn't have a choice. I was afraid of Dad so this was now one of the many chores I had to do around this place that we now called home.

The city kids were now to become country kids. Our new way of life couldn't have been more different from what we had left behind. We missed the friends we had made in Detroit. Suddenly, the bar didn't seem so bad. Everyone except Dad missed our life in Belgium.

In the United States, we were gone all day in the summer with no supervision. Amusing ourselves and staying out of the way. From the time I was ll years old, my life was very different. Corrie and I were up at three or four in the morning to rent and clean boats. Depending on the weather, this schedule began in April and could have gone on until October. This task took a lot of strength and energy. It was basically not the kind of job children ages ten to fourteen should be doing. In the daytime, when we finished with the boats, we cleaned cottages and took care of the lawn. We discovered that people on vacation tend to be quite messy and are not good at looking after a property that does not belong to them. We marveled that no one had taught many of these people how to leave a place as tidy as they found it. This was exhausting work and beyond what children are capable of doing, but we did it. We got very little sleep and lifting boats, cleaning cottages, and sometimes mowing lawns really did tax our bodies. What I hated the most was weeding the gravel parking lot. My hands were bloody and calloused from this activity. Dad just didn't want to use weed killer. All three of us grew up with serious back and muscle problems which I attribute to lifting weights that exceeded what young bodies could handle.

Our small house had a small kitchen, a dining room, and a tiny living room. There was one small bathroom and we all had to learn to take our turn….except for Dad. He didn't care whether there was a line…if he had to go…he went first. He also took a lot of time in the bathroom, usually reading a book. The worst part of all this was that he really knew how to smell the place up. Wow! Since there was only one bedroom, the three of us girls had to sleep on the enclosed, uninsulated porch, which wasn't a huge problem in the summer, except for the mosquitoes, but the winter was another issue, since we had no central heating system at all. I was grateful to sleep with Corrie, since we often woke up with snow on our blankets and staying warm called for a lot of cuddling. We felt sorry for Ria as she slept alone and was always cold. Corrie and I invited her to join us, but she said she preferred her own bed, even though it was cold. I didn't think she ever warmed up. The house was kept warm by an oil heater and the kitchen was warmed by the coal stove. We were happy to have electricity most of the time and also a party line telephone.

There were ten neighbors connected on this party line and everyone could hear everyone else's conversations. At times, this could be fun, but at other times, you really didn't want the whole neighborhood to hear what was said. I have to admit that Corrie and I sometimes listened to the neighbors' conversations and actually got to know some of them in this way. We had to remain very quiet and not giggle; however, we sometimes erupted with laughter. Once we got caught as the eavesdroppers that we were, Mom made it very clear that there was to be no listening in on other people's calls. We agreed. However, we missed the stories we heard.

During our first year at the camp, we begged Dad for a dog, and he came up with a very young female dog, a golden retriever, named Goldie. It wasn't a very imaginative name, but it suited her as she was a beautiful light gold color. She was wonderful. She was loving and playful and greeted us with vigorous, loud, joyous excitement each time she saw us. It was like we were the most important people in her life. I loved her enthusiastic greetings and loved playing with her. Dad said that she was an outside dog, and that meant she would NEVER be allowed inside. We said we understood what "outside" meant. However, I don't think we really understood all the ramifications of this statement. We also did not realize that she had not been spayed; in fact, we had no idea what being spayed meant. We had no idea how dogs get pregnant, how to prevent pregnancy in dogs, and what it would mean if a very young, outside dog got pregnant. We were ignorant when it came to human and animal bodily functions. We never had a dog before. It was not long before she mysteriously became pregnant. It was wintertime, and we finally understood what Dad meant by "outside dog." I never dreamed that the poor thing could never be let in the house, even when it was bitter cold.

Goldie gave birth to twelve puppies, and Jake said that there was no way that she could feed all of them. She was just too young.

"Please let her in the house…she is so young and it is very cold outside…please…she has a lot of puppies and they will all freeze." We begged, cried, and pleaded to let the poor animal in the house. The answer was a very angry "NO."

Goldie was so weak and I even thought she was in pain. We made a bed for Goldie and her puppies in the coal shed, and Corrie and I stayed out with them. It was so cold, but we spent many nights outside. We hoped that we could help Goldie, but she just couldn't feed them all and our attempts at feeding them did not work. Jake ended up drowning eight of the puppies, thinking that maybe the four strongest could survive. Although we understood what Jake was trying to do, we were grief-stricken, and cried and begged for another solution. Finally, we had to accept what Jake recommended. We begged Dad: "Please, please, can we bring Goldie and the four remaining pups inside where they could be warm." We begged for a doctor. He refused.

Corrie shrieked, "You're a terrible person; you just don't care for this living being." Everyone froze…no one spoke…Dad looked stunned. All that I could hear were sobs. We all slowly exited the room. I was shocked that Dad had not hit us. I thought that we would get it later. This was the first time I heard anyone scream at Dad and I admired Corrie for doing so. Surprisingly, no one was punished.

Although it was bitter cold, Corrie and I stayed outside with Goldie and the four puppies, but they all died by the end of the week. Corrie and I were inconsolable. I felt such intense grief; I just couldn't believe what happened. I was shocked by what I thought of as Dad's cruelty. I never felt so helpless in my life.

We wanted to have a funeral, but Dad had Jake bury the dogs. I thought about Goldie for a long time and wondered if there was anything else we could have done. I felt anger I had never felt, sadness I did not know existed, and vowed not to count on Dad for anything important again. I was also disappointed in Mom, as she had not intervened or tried to help in any way. She remained quiet throughout the weeks that this tragedy unfolded. We went to her and begged and pleaded and cried, but to no avail. She was not going to fight for us and Goldie. Dad had not wanted to pay for a veterinarian, but I decided that if this happened again, I would find a way to pay for a doctor to come.

After a number of months, we got another dog, a springer spaniel named Freckles. He was a male, so we don't have to worry about pregnancy. He is a wonderful dog, but I'm finding myself ever so careful when it comes to attaching myself to another living creature. The pain of Goldie's loss is still fresh and I need to take care when it comes to opening my heart. Freckles seemed sensitive to my reluctance. He is a good dog. 1951

A COUNTRY SCHOOL

When we moved to Canada, I was in the sixth grade, Corrie was in fifth grade, and Ria in eighth grade. The school we attended was a small, brick country schoolhouse with one room and a large potbelly stove, bathrooms with no doors on the stalls, and a cloakroom. The stove was the only heat in the building. There were some large wooden desks and many wooden tables of all sizes that the students sat around. The large room sat about fifty children from kindergarten to eighth grade. It was a cozy space, but could use a little paint and a little more care.

There were some books, but not like in the Grosse Pointe Schools and there was no library. I was used to seeing students' work on the walls, but there was very little considering how many children studied in this large room. There were several kids with special needs and one young girl named Annette who had Down's syndrome. These children, and especially Annette, were teased a lot by the other kids. There was only one teacher, Mrs. Callop, for the whole school. She seemed overwhelmed when it came to stopping the hurtful teasing. She really cracked the whip to get the kids to sit still. Chaos in this school was very short-lived, as Mrs. Callop was a top sergeant controlling her troops. She had a variety of punishments. You could kneel in the front of the room with a heavy book in each hand as your arms were outstretched, you could kneel on stones in front of the room, or you could kneel in front of the room and wear a dunce cap. The other punishment that no one wanted was the strap in the cloakroom, applied resoundingly on your hands or backside while your classmates counted the number of whacks you could tolerate before crying. We could really hear the loud whacks when the strap connected and we all groaned and held ourselves tight with each crack of the strap.

This school did not resemble anything similar to what we were expecting or had experienced in the past. However, I challenged myself to prove that I could succeed anywhere. I was not going to let this backwoods school slow me down. I knew that my education would depend on what I chose to learn…it was my responsibility. No one would do the work for me. I felt challenged.

Out of boredom, I started on my own brand of education. I bought a subscription to *Reader's Digest* and used the vocabulary lists to create a game for myself. I was to use all of these words in one essay and use them correctly. Also, the meaning of the essay had to be coherent and cohesive. In other words, the essay had to make sense, in spite of the fact that the words in the list did not necessarily fit together. This was one pleasant way I could occupy my time. I even worked on this task while waiting in the morning for the boat renters to come. I joined the Audubon Society and learned about the bird and water species around our camp. I drew charcoal drawings and painted oil pictures of all of the critters I could find. I read all I could get my hands on relating to any and all topics. This was how I spent what little spare time I could find. My focus was learning all that I could. My goal was to ultimately get out of this home and make something of myself and I knew that education would be my way out.

From my diary: I'm struggling to find things, events, and people to feel good about. I'm not able to form many friendships as I have very little in common with the kids in school. I have one friend, Patsy, but she told me she is moving to Texas. Even though I don't know her very well, I will miss her. She says we can write, but I know that will not happen. Friends from Europe promised that but they do

For the moment, I was stuck in this one-room school. There were few books, no laboratory for science, no music, and only one teacher to pull everything together. The punishments may sound like child abuse, but it wasn't really horrible. It took an incredible amount of work for Mrs. Callop to control this herd of kids, and she did it. She used what was available to her and did her best. She had me teaching the younger children and Ria also taught. I discovered that the best way to master a subject is to teach it. Our education in math and science was definitely lacking, but our teacher made up for it with literature. We had to memorize a substantial poem each week and I loved being able to recite these poems. She seemed to like the Romantic poets best, and we read many of them. History was interesting because it was quite different from what we had learned in American schools, as Britain and Canada won all the wars, according to the class discussions.

The emphasis on poetry in school encouraged me to write poems and I did write many while in Canada. Some sounded like the ravings of a hysteric, but all came from deep in my soul. As I read them now, I'm struck by the deep passion and depression evident in the words, images, and cadence. I could at least express myself on paper. I felt a growing struggle and yearning within me to be loved and touched by Mom and Dad, to be close to someone. While I wanted the freedom to express my thoughts and feelings without the worry of recrimination, I was afraid to open myself up for ridicule. I kept my poetry as my secret. I was surprised to learn recently that Corrie had not read my poems when we were teens. The following poem speaks of my struggles to control my rage at my father, for distance, for closeness, for autonomy, and for a desperation for love.

TORN

Your voice sounds in my ears -

Shall I never be capable of tuning you out?

Of exorcizing you?

I hate your growing domination of my soul

As my feelings for you become more transparent.

No longer can I decide what will be spoken of

Or what emotions will be made visible?

Loss of control-

My greatest fear-

With the gods

I can tolerate

That futile struggle

Familiar to all their puppets.

Though forever a malcontent

I have accepted this clown-like role

Sport for the Immortals.

And, through lethargy,

Have even achieved some semblance of autonomy.

But your presence bewilders me.

The gods did not disturb my world

And I reciprocated

A blessedly dull, uncomplicated arrangement.

But now there is no peace,

You stand before me each moment of my day

While I become more helpless than before,

The scraps you toss me sharpen my appetite

and NOW I AM RULED BY ABSURD DESIRES

TO BE HELD AND TAKEN CARE OF

Feelings I can no longer deny-

I fall victim to your powers

Relinquish my freedom

And gamble for my life. (1952)

In my home, we did not speak the truth. In order to get some of our needs met, we said what was expected of us. We relinquished our freedom. When we left Belgium, we gave up on the truth. When my father came into my life, he took over. He was the power and Mom had given up. Things went his way. The hugs that I identified with love were gone. I don't really know why I felt hungry for them, but I kept silent. I grieved the loss of the closeness I felt in Belgium. I was alone. I was also beginning to believe that God had deserted me. At home, it was hard to feel "real," but at school, it was easier to express what I felt without needing to defend what I said. With all of the problems the school presented, I still felt this place would be my saving grace. School was my new refuge, my garden of safety. 1952

The Camp, a flood and Jake

SS #8 Dover School all 8 grades

Kristy Corrie

Ria's wedding

The school, SS #8 Dover, was in a strictly agricultural area, so many of the children came to school sporadically in spring and fall because of planting and harvesting. Attendance at school was dependent on the weather and the season. Bad weather and winter meant high school attendance; warm weather and heavy rain meant high attendance; warm weather and sun meant very low attendance. What was being taught at school was not very relevant, but the weather was. It was country living. A few of the farmers were wealthy and most very poor. The children of the wealthy farmers tended to come to school consistently. Children of the poor came more sporadically. Many of the families made their living on the lake and worked in jobs related to fishing and hunting. The majority of the families were quite poor and did not seem to value education. So the end result was that many of the students were behind in academic achievement and needed a lot of one-on-one help. That was where my sisters and I came in handy. We tutored on a one-on-one basis and taught classes. Many students dropped out to help on the farm when they reached fifth or sixth grade.

Teaching subjects is a great way to learn, and I loved learning in this fashion. If you can explain a concept to someone else, chances are you have really integrated it yourself. Being singled out as a teacher's helper does wonders for self-esteem but does very little when it comes to relating to fellow students. Forming friendships became even more complicated.

A challenge for me was helping a student like thirteen-year-old Annette, who was seriously handicapped intellectually. All subjects were difficult for her, but she loved to be read to and worked hard on first-grade math. When she succeeded at something, she clapped her hands with glee. Her joy felt contagious. I loved her reaction and her joyous exuberance. That is what made it so wonderful to help others learn.

When I graduated from eighth grade, I was at the top of my class of two. The same was true for Ria and Corrie. By now, I was excelling in English and had no issues expressing myself; however, I shared very few personal feelings and still kept to myself. My sisters and I would speak nostalgically, amongst ourselves, about Belgium and the life and family we left behind. Flemish represented a part of my life that had ceased to exist, as we were all forgetting our native language with lack of use. This loss felt like a part of my soul was disappearing into a past shrouded by a fog of disuse.

I try unsuccessfully to put the past away, to hide from the images of war and destruction that confront me when I slow down and stop running. They find me in my dreams. I can't understand how I can long for a world where I was terrified most of the time, just to have the memory of the family togetherness. What's so wonderful about wartime experiences that I wanted them back in Canada? I definitely feel confused. 1952

My sisters and I either walked home or rode our bicycles. It was about three miles from school to home on a dirt road. In the winter, we sometimes ice skated to school on the creek that ran next to the road. It was a wonderfully peaceful way to go to school. Everything looked beautiful as the bushes and trees along the creek were bejeweled with the early morning frost. The sun would strike the ice and the frost would reflect back rainbows of colors. I loved this journey, especially when it was not bitter cold.

Ria, one morning, fell through the ice while skating. We heard her screams:

"Help, help, I need help, don't let me die."

"I'm coming…we'll get you out. Hold onto the ice and try to get up on it."

"I'm trying, but it keeps breaking off."

We stretched out on the ice and got a large piece of wood over to her. Gradually, she got herself onto the solid parts of the ice with our help. It was a challenge for us to free her from the water. We were all so wet and cold, but Ria was soaked through.

"I'm so cold," she said as she trembled in the freezing air.

"We have to get her to the nearest home quickly. The intense cold is dangerous," I said, glancing around to see what neighbor was closest.

Corrie skated to the Smith home to ask the dad to come and help us get Ria there. It was a very small home owned by a family with a very mean boy and Annette, the Down syndrome girl. George, the dad, worked as a guide on one of our boats, so he knew us. He took us home. We definitely learned from this experience not to skate where the ice might be thin and what to look for to make sure the ice was thick enough. The city girls were getting some very fast lessons in country living.

In the spring, at a time when I was homesick, Corrie was riding her bicycle to school by herself. Ria was now going to Wallaceburg District High School. Riding home, Corrie concentrated on her new lunch box which threatened to bounce out of her carrier. Not paying attention to where she was going, she did not see or hear the giant tractor coming directly in front of her.

Other kids yelled, "There's a tractor coming; move to the side."

But Corrie was in her own dream world. The tractor hit her and rode over her bike and her legs. Her beautiful bike was done for. Everyone thought this was also the end of Corrie, and kids ran to the nearest home to call Dad. Jake had been driving to our home when he drove up to the scene. Everyone present was incredibly worried and several people took Corrie to the hospital. Once he was found, Dad, in his typical way, was furious and angry about the idea of going to Chatham to the Emergency Room and then having to wait for the medics to check her out.

He screamed at the Emergency Room staff: "I don't have all day and I don't care if you don't have a room available to check her out; do it here now!"

Corrie pleaded: "Not here in the waiting room, Dad, please, there are lots of people here, please! It's embarrassing…please!"

The doctor did what Dad wanted. He seemed immune to the fact that Corrie was an eleven-year-old girl who did not want to lift up her dress to show where the tractor had ridden over her. Corrie was totally humiliated and shamed. There was no consideration for how she felt. All that seemed to matter was what Dad wanted and what was convenient for him. He could even bully the doctors. The doctor was thoughtless and totally inconsiderate; he agreed to examine an eleven-year-old girl in the waiting room with other patients around. I was furious with Dad and with the doctor. Corrie had the imprints of the tractor tires on her upper thighs, but she must have fallen in a rut on the road. She had no broken bones, and we were grateful for that. This experience in the ER was probably more traumatic for Corrie than the actual accident. All three of us were upset by this invasion of personal space and the lack of recognition by the men involved, that privacy matters, even for a child. Once more the question of "Who can you trust?" had taken center stage. I also wondered if there was anyone around who would look after our well-being. If you can't be safe in a hospital where people are supposed to be able to help you, where can you be safe? I was surprised that there was no one in that ER who valued a child's need over the narcissistic demands of a nasty adult who was complaining about having to wait for fifteen minutes for a room to become available.

I need to find ways to stay in touch with the good in the world. I know it is there and I want to be part of it.

Dawn and sunset are my favorite times as the colors and sounds of the world around me turn magical. I love to walk the berms by the marshes, especially when the sky becomes brilliant and the whole marsh seems to come alive. At dawn, the sounds of the birds and other wildlife are like a symphony. Every living thing around me seems in harmony. It might be noisy but there is no conflict. In the evening, the frogs and toads rumble to life. I bathe in the sense of peace around me. 1952

I became enthralled with the Audubon Society and collected all the pictures I could afford of birds and other wildlife from the area. I was interested in learning about the various habitats and became very concerned about environmental issues. I did a lot of photography, drawing, painting, and writing poetry while on my walks along the marshes. I loved the shapes of the reeds and the soft colors of the flowers of the wetlands. I felt peace in the marshlands that I did not feel in my home. I felt close to God on those berms, and prayed for divine intervention. I did not understand how God could create a world so beautiful that it could turn in a moment into hell on earth. But beyond providing the glorious marshland, God's positive intervention did not come.

Lake St. Clair

Lake St. Clair can be a wild, treacherous body of water. It is relatively shallow, and this contributes to the violence of the weather on this smallest of the Great Lakes. Storms come up quickly, frequently with little or no warning, and they often claim victims. We rented boats to boat people and to boating neophytes. The latter often took risks and were oblivious to the dangers involved. The former often assumed they understood and could predict the lake's moods, sometimes with tragic outcomes.

I am thirteen; it is a Saturday in the summer. The skies are clear blue with no clouds in sight. The air is warm and the wind is gentle, almost still. Suddenly, the skies change as the wind increases from a gentle breeze to a roaring hurricane and the rain comes with a force that is painful as it pelts against my skin. When the storm is over, I look outside and see a number of Provincial Police officers rushing to the dock. I ran out to see what was going on. I stood in shock as I saw what's happening. Slowly and reverently, they brought the bodies of a family of five onto the land and laid them on what looked like black plastic which was covering the wet grass. All had drowned in the violent storm. I can still see these small bodies as they lay so silently on the bright green grass. Are they dead? They can't be dead! I can't believe what I am seeing! They are lined up on the soft carpet of green grass. I stare at their very young faces and try to comprehend what has happened. It is so unfair.1952

"Why did it happen?"

Their beautiful, bright play clothes, still wet from the storm, were so out of place in this somber scene. The children looked like they were sleeping peacefully and would wake up any moment as the noise around them increased. I wanted to touch the face of the youngest child, to move his wet hair from his eyes, but I couldn't move. I prayed that this was all a dream. But it wasn't. The Provincial Police were there attempting to find out what happened. I had interacted with the family earlier in the day, when the weather was clear and sunny. The little kids had been so excited about going to the lake. One said, "I'm going to catch lots of fish and Daddy says we can eat them for dinner."

Another youngster told me proudly, "I can put the worm on the hook. Daddy showed me how." As the children spoke to me, their father beamed with pride.

I told the police officer that they had put their boat in the water at our boat launch. I kept saying that maybe I should have warned them that the lake was dangerous, but I had no idea how very dangerous. The Dad was a grownup; he would know these things and he would know what to do. I should have reminded them more strongly to use life preservers. I thought fathers would know how to look after their children.

The policeman was kind and said several times, "This wasn't your fault. You had nothing to do with this…Don't blame yourself. I repeatedly told myself that I was not responsible for this tragedy, but I did not feel convinced. I told myself that even the police officers who interviewed me were clear that I had no responsibility in this tragedy. Initially I felt my feelings were frozen, as was my body. I couldn't move. I couldn't make a sound. Gradually, as I tuned into what was happening around me, I became aware that this was not a dream. This tragedy had actually happened. I began to sob. Tears rolled down my cheeks. I stood there, taking it all in. Faintly, I heard Mom calling me. I turned and saw her on the porch. She waved for me to go to her. When I reached her, she grabbed me and I put my arms around her and we held onto each other until my body held no more tears.

I mourned this family and dreamt for years about this horror. It is hard for a young person to put such experiences in perspective. Children tend to be quite fearful of death, and I was no different. I wondered where the spirits of these children were now that their bodies were no longer viable. I pondered the question of whether there was life after death. Did their souls enter some other living being or perhaps they moved to some alternate universe? I had so very many questions. So many fantasies. There was so much I did not understand. I did not want to believe that death was permanent. I couldn't believe that the children wouldn't just get up from their sleep and again begin to play. I still think about this. This tragedy stays with me in both my waking and sleeping life.

There were other deaths at the camp. I remember a fisherman running into the house to tell us that his friend had died on the lake. The old man was still sitting upright in the boat, but you could easily tell that he was dead. He looked very gray and had a puzzled, pained look on his face.

Mom told me: "Go into the boat and cover him up with a blanket. We can't leave him uncovered like this."

I yelled: "But Mom, he's dead, it's yucky...I don't want to touch him."

I felt overwhelmed and afraid, but Mom said she couldn't go into a boat; she had never been in a boat, she was terrified of water. I don't remember whether I covered him up or whether Corrie and I did it together, but we did it. I definitely felt traumatized by this and other such experiences. I saw this man's face in my nightmares for many years afterwards.

I wondered: "Why did God give life and then take it away?" It was easier to accept the death of the old man, but the children. "Why did they have to die?"

The lake was fickle in many ways. For several years, the water level was extremely high which meant we had to rebuild our docks and basically raise them up to accommodate the higher water level. During another year, the water level was low and our higher docks were a problem. So we now had to lower them. We also created some berms to protect us from being submerged. However, we still had several episodes of raging storms when we had lots of water all over. The cottages were flooded and our yard was impassable. We couldn't even get over the bridge to the road; however, even if we could have, the road itself was completely submerged. We were stuck in our home for days and then we had a very difficult and messy job of cleaning up.

"I can't believe the mud and junk everywhere! We need more help!"

It was so hard for me to put one foot in front of the other when it came to cleaning up. I felt it was hopeless. I did not feel up to the task. I've seldom felt that a job was too big for me, but here, I really felt overwhelmed. My tears took charge for a while, but the job was done and I moved on.

In my attempts to recover from the traumas my new way of life brought to me, I began to write more poetry. Somehow or other, I managed to save many of these poems and they provide a window into my mind. They are the ravings and visceral impressions of a very depressed adolescent. I include them in this memoir as they are the most direct path to my adolescent self. I have to admit that I am personally surprised at how intense my young self's feelings are. I wonder if anything would have been different if I had shown my poems to someone, not my Mother or Father, but someone who might have been helpful.

WARNINGS

Never-ending storms

Forever threats

Forever fears

Always that dark cloud

Harbinger of impending doom.

Growing denser

More foreboding

As the earth moves on.

While I,

The constant spectator,

Watch from my isolated perch.

First the drizzle…

Then wind and rain and lightning…

Finally destruction. (1953)

My young mind is feeling as though it is in free-fall and I am increasingly depressed. Nightmares, which have always been a problem for me, possess the night, but I continue to be grateful that Corrie is there for me.

Corrie later tells me she was grateful for my presence too, as she was also struggling. I was questioning everything that was happening to me. We seldom spoke of problems, and I focused on being optimistic. I did not understand why bad things kept happening and we just did not talk about real issues. We were so

106

close but oh, so far. Perhaps, had we been able to share our thoughts and feelings, life might have been easier for us.

I feel like all I can do is watch Mom, who has been my rock. How is she dealing with all of the difficulties we are faced with? I wonder how long she can keep going at the pace she is working. I couldn't bear to lose her. 1953

Mom worked from dawn to late at night and much of what she did was very physically taxing. I also felt the tension between Mom and Dad, and wondered what would happen with the two of them. She sometimes expressed her feelings, but she did so gingerly. I don't know if she was afraid that Dad would hurt her physically. He was quick to strike out at us, and I worried that he was not able to control himself and Mom could not stop him. I was terrified when Dad picked up the pot of stew and smashed it against the floor because he felt slighted about something. Anything could set him off and there was no way of predicting his response. I tried to talk to Mom but she would become overwhelmed with guilt and anxiety and start crying. I would have done anything to keep her from sadness. More and more, she didn't know what to do. I think she was both physically and emotionally exhausted. In Europe, she always seemed to know how to solve problems. She was in charge. She had friends and people she could talk to and confide in. Now, she was alone. There was no one she could share her fears with or get comfort from. She seemed as confused as we were. She was no longer my rock. I felt increasingly that I could not depend on Mom. She was not the same Mom who saw us through the war. She had also lost her moorings. I worried that she would die.

We finally found a church to go to on Sunday and this was helping in providing something familiar we could hold on to. The ritual was blessedly similar to the churches in Detroit and Belgium.

We didn't make it as regularly as in the past, but at least we tried. Corrie and I joined a group of kids studying for Confirmation. Again, we didn't make all of the meetings, but we made enough to finish the program. At this point, I didn't feel the peace that I used to feel in church. I didn't understand my feelings, especially depression and anger, and I felt them more intensely in church. I was frightened by my anger at God. It did not feel right to be this angry with God. Several times, my anxiety grew so intense that I passed out during the service. I am incredibly embarrassed when this happens.

A BABY - 1952

I was thirteen and Mom told us that she was pregnant.

"Oh my gosh, will it be a boy or a girl? When will it come?"

"We'll know in time. Keep in mind that I just found out I was pregnant. I'm glad you're excited. I am, too."

I was thrilled at the idea of a baby in the family. Corrie and Ria felt the same. I went into overtime knitting and crocheting baby clothes. This was going to be the cutest baby of all time and also the best dressed. We were all so excited, and even Mom seemed less depressed and started looking forward to a new baby. Mom was forty-six and considered "old" by her doctor. She did well; at least she never complained throughout most of her pregnancy and that was surprising since she always worked so hard. She got really big with the baby and I was surprised about the changes I saw in her body.

The last couple months of her pregnancy was duck hunting season and Mom always prepared dinners for up to twenty hunters per night. Her dinners were not simple meals. They often consisted of some of the game the hunters had bagged, fancy potatoes, veggies, salad, bread, dessert, and wine. This was an incredible amount of work for her, but she continued to say that she enjoyed the meal preparation and appreciated the praise she got at the end of the night. This was in addition to Mom doing the laundry for the cottages using a wringer washer and hanging sheets to dry outside, even in the winter. We helped with laundry as much as we could and did all of the dishes for these meals. While doing the dishes, we would sing and harmonize. I loved those times. I still enjoy doing the dishes, and remembering the fun with my sisters.

We worried that Mom was working herself to death. Her body and her legs were incredibly swollen and we wondered if that was normal. She was very quiet and kept all of her thoughts to herself. She kept saying all was fine with her, but I had trouble believing her. I knew she did not share how she felt physically with anyone. I knew that what she was experiencing could not be easy, but she did not reach out for help. Dad would spend his time socializing and drinking with the hunters. He could be charming and definitely won over the customers. He just did not help with the work. He also did not see to it that her workload was reduced…he just did not seem to notice that she was struggling. I noticed that the work was getting to be too much for her, but she continued with: "I'm okay, it won't be long for the baby to come and then I'll feel more normal again. Don't worry."

We worried and did what we could to lighten Mom's load. Her body got bigger and bigger with the baby, but she continued to do the work that needed to be done. The laundry and the dinners were the most difficult chores but she would not let us take over, and I'm not so sure that we could have taken over.

After one such dinner, Mom went to the hospital in labor. The hospital was in Chatham and her doctor was called. She had apparently been in labor all evening and she finally had Dad take her to the hospital when dinner and clean-up was over and she was ready to deliver the baby. But even though Mom had called ahead, and told the triage person how long she had been in labor and that she was ready to deliver, the doctor still was not there. He told the nurses to keep Mom's legs closed and delay the delivery. He came eighteen hours later and had been drinking, based on reports of how he smelled. We later learned that Mom lost her baby boy as he was strangled by the birth cord. She almost lost her life.

Dad made us go to school since we had no news and there was nothing we could do while he was at the hospital with Mom. We were terrified of losing Mom and didn't want to go, but he insisted. We heard how dire the situation was from the kids in school who had been listening on our party line to a conversation between Dad and Jake. We were in school and the kids who had listened in were cruel and teased us unmercifully. They insisted that both Mom and the baby were dead.

"Na, na, na, your Mom is dead and so is her baby! Naa na…"

I remember that during music class, the whole school was singing "It Is No Secret What God Can Do," and I cried to myself: "God...can't you do something? Now is the time to do something! I need you to do something! Please do something! You can do everything!" Tears rolled down my cheeks as I prayed and tried to sing.. I felt helpless and alone. I looked over at Corrie and I could see that her cheeks were also wet with tears. I wanted to be near her and feel her hand in mine. I did not want to be alone. I felt I was in a hostile environment trying to deal with what I feared would be the loss of the most important person in my life. There was no one I could turn to. I just couldn't believe what the kids had said.

I kept praying that God would undo whatever had happened and that the baby would be alive and that Mom would be fine. I tried to bargain with God. I could think of nothing but Mom and the baby. I prayed very hard but nothing changed the truth. We had to wait until the end of school to hear what had actually happened. The whole day had been a nightmare for me. When we got home, we learned that the baby was dead, BUT Mom was alive. God came through and we got to keep Mom. I was so happy about this but I was angry at God that the baby was dead.

Dad said, "I held the baby and he was a perfect little boy with dark, curly hair. He was beautiful and I'm so glad I could hold him. He looked like he was asleep."

Dad, who had mainly shown us anger in the past, had tears in his eyes. I hadn't even believed that he had wanted the baby. I had never seen him sad and this frightened me. He looked defeated and worn. Mom came home; her spirit sucked out of her. She was quiet, sad, and tearful. We never got to see the baby.

I asked, "Will we have a funeral for the baby?"

No one answered. We never spoke about this tragedy again, but our collective sadness permeated all our lives. The baby clothes, furniture, and toys silently disappeared. The baby's name was Edward, after Mom's brother. His name was only spoken once while I was young. There was no funeral and no way to say goodbye. Silence prevailed. My hopes, dreams, and love for this child evaporated, as did my tears. I grieved. When I think of him today, I still grieve.

TEARS

Fragile life gone

So soft and white

Dark curls frame

The delicate face

Still, Still

Tiny motionless body

Wrapped in white

Cradled in Daddy's arms

Little boy gone

Tears flow

We Grieve. (1953)

OFF TO EUROPE FOR MOM AND DAD

Mom's depression continued and deepened. She was a shell of the person she used to be. She was lost and we all worried about her. She said very little and never spoke of her loss. She went through the motions of life. In February 1953, Dad decided to take Mom back to Europe and family. He hoped this would help alleviate her sense of hopelessness.

They were gone for three months, and during that time, fifteen-year-old Ria was in charge. Jake lived nearby and we could go to him if we needed someone or if we needed a ride somewhere. We were given some money for food, but we had to figure out how to get the groceries. None of us were skilled at cooking, so we had a lot to learn. The first week, Ria spent a good deal of our money on onions, potatoes, and apples. Ria tried to make onion soup, but cooked the onions, peels and all.

"Oh boy, our first meal alone. What is it? Oh God, you're supposed to peel the onions and you have to do more than just toss them in water. This is terrible."

We laughed and laughed at Ria, but she didn't take our laughter in good humor; instead, she got furious and grabbed Corrie and threw her across the room. Wow, we were not expecting her rage. Ria really does not escalate to violence; in fact, she seldom gets angry. Corrie got a cut on her head when she landed against the wall. She didn't go to school the next day as Jake wanted to be sure her head injury was not serious. We both apologized to Ria for laughing at her and decided to be more careful when we laughed at some of the ignorant things we did. Not everyone feels friendly toward laughter that is intended to highlight our stupid behavior and make us feel like fools.

The food we made was absolutely terrible. We decided our food skills could only go up from there. We did learn something about cooking and made some foods we liked. We even learned to follow recipes sometimes. We missed Mom but were determined to take care of ourselves. We kept busy, did our school work, kept the house up, and did a lot of reading during what felt like a very long winter. Mom telephoned us once in that time period, and she seemed worried about us. We reassured her that all was well with us and that she did not need to worry. We made it until they came back, but ended up fully appreciating the work Mom put into the family. We were definitely sick of onions, potatoes, and apples. We wanted Mom's food.

Since I was such an introvert, I had few friends I spent any time with, and I had no sleepovers with girlfriends, where important information about growing up is often shared. My sisters and I talked, but we didn't talk about changes in our bodies. Mom avoided talk of bodily development and puberty. I think she believed we would just instinctively know. I had no idea that my body would make any changes without my awareness or consent. Ria had somehow become aware of what puberty was all about, but she did not share any of the information she had learned. She was silent about everything. I loved science and especially biology but was still minimally informed about the processes involved in maturation. However I never dreamed that any of the limited information I had read about applied to me and specifically to MY body. While Mom was gone to Europe, I started my period, and, of course, believed the worst: I was dying. I locked myself up in a cabin attached to our house and cried. I felt terrible. I thought I was dying and I wanted Mom. I had no idea what to do. Jake's girlfriend, Margie, finally found me and gave me some of the information I needed: "You're not dying; this is a normal part of growing up. This will happen once per month. Get used to it."

I am shaken and traumatized, not only by my first period, but by my lack of knowledge. Here is something else I am not in control of. What a horrible thing to happen to girls. It's not fair. Margie says boys don't have to deal with this. I feel deep shame, both in relating to my body and because I had been so ignorant. How could I have kept myself so thoroughly in the dark? I am growing up, but feel so lost and inadequate. The world and I are not on the same wavelength. I also feel anger at Mom and Ria. How could they have neglected to give me vital information? 1953

On looking back, I realized that I had seen Ria with pads and had asked her what they were for. She said, "Oh, they're for my feet."

That made no sense to me but I let the response go, never dreaming in a million years what they were really for. Corrie also started her period during the time Mom was gone, but she learned from my experience and had some information from her friends and Ria. I was happy for her about that. I felt like an idiot for knowing so little about my body. Who could I trust to tell me the truth? Even my inner guide was out of tune with the events happening in my life. It seemed that even though I was great at asking questions, I was not asking the right questions and definitely not getting the answers I needed. I wish there was someone who could help me sort out some of the questions I have about life.

CRACKS

This table was much higher.

The house was larger.

You're deceiving me.

Nothing is as it was,

As it is,

As it will be.

The house I know had no cracks,

No dark and filthy halls.

Why is this place so cold?

Who planted weeds in my garden?

The ground is trampled and hard.

My garden exploded.

With the joyous laughter of children,

With the omnipresence of lilacs,

With the simple beauty of dandelions.

This is not my garden!

Who planted these weeds?

Where is my garden? (1954)

HIGH SCHOOL

It was finally time for me to go to high school. I was very excited about this change. Now, I could take the bus and go to a school that more clearly matched my idea of a place of learning..this school had a library. Wallaceburg District High School was about forty-five minutes away from our home. The bus went all over hell and creation. At least, that was what it felt like. I loved the school and had my first crush on a teacher. Mr. Beecroft taught chemistry, AND he was in charge of the photography club. Wow...when could I join? I learned a lot about photography and about developing pictures, but most important of all, I got to be in the darkroom with Mr. Beecroft.

"Maybe I can accidentally touch his hands, oh my goodness. I get to spend time with him."

Thank God he was a good person and nothing bad happened, but my imagination was a bit nuts. I loved that time, and in retrospect, I loved that I was innocent and felt safe and was safe. My favorite classes were literature and history, and I continued to love these subjects throughout my life. School always felt safe to me. I enjoyed learning and did very well in school. I was a nerd and happy to be one. I got to know a few people, but didn't stay long enough to develop friendships that were lasting. I remember the name of one friend I had, Patsy, and she moved away to Texas the first year we were in Canada. I never heard from her again and I didn't try to contact her. Corrie is still in touch with one friend from our Canada days. Adele was a classmate at S.S. No. 8 Dover, our country school, and they continued their relationship to this day. Corrie has always done a masterful job of staying connected to people she likes.

Social life…what was it? We related to the customers who came to the camp. There were very few children in the neighborhood and we had nothing in common with these neighbors. Corrie became friends with a boy whose family was renting a cottage of ours for two weeks. He was around her age, probably thirteen or fourteen. The family was going to a dance at the Catholic church in Pain Court and the boy asked Corrie if she could go. She asked Dad, but he was already fairly drunk and he absolutely lost all self-control when she and the boy asked. Dad's eyes seemed to pop out from his head as he relinquished any attempt to control himself. . His face was red, his jaw set in anger, and he moved with a speed I had never seen in him.

He screamed: "No, no boy is going out with you, I'll kill him!"

Then he ran to get his shotgun and started chasing the boy and Corrie around the campground. Everyone was terrified and both the boy and Corrie were hysterical. Luckily, Mom was nearby and she got to Dad and grabbed his gun. Corrie didn't go, and we were all afraid to ask to go to social events, and definitely not with a boy. I was shocked at what Dad did, and I was even more surprised that the family of the boy did not call the police. I secretly hoped they would call the police and that Dad might learn not to run around chasing people with a gun. I was afraid of how Dad would react if the police were called, but I still wanted that to happen. It did not happen. I had hoped that Mom would do more than just grab Dad's gun, but nothing more was said of this event.

Dad did this shotgun thing another time. The school bus stopped in the parking lot once and the driver let all the kids get off and said we could play ball for ten minutes.

Dad came out screaming, "Get out of here! What are you doing here?"

He waved his shotgun and it was the shortest ten minutes ever, as everyone scrambled back on the bus and headed for the bridge away from us. I was incredibly embarrassed by his behavior. Mom confronted him but it did no good. The driver did not notify the school or the police.

Ria did her socializing at school, but not in the safest way. She used to ride around with friends at lunch in their cars even though she was not allowed this privilege. One time, while they were riding around, she fell out of the car and had some minor injuries. Mom and Dad were called and they were furious. Ria continued to find opportunities to hang out with friends, often leading to problems. When I think about the craziness of these times, I am not surprised that relationships have been difficult for all three of us. She started smoking at this time and I believe this is where she began using some drugs and alcohol.

We did find some ways to have fun. I wrote a lot of poetry and read many books. I also enjoyed painting. As a family, we often played card games of all sorts. We had rousing games of canasta, hearts, and many other card games. We loved Monopoly and board games. I tended to be a sore loser and would sometimes lose my temper when I didn't win. My sisters had easier times when they lost. I was grateful that they continued to be willing to play with me and I did try to control my temper. I became aware of how important it was for me to learn to lose gracefully.

Getting angry does not help; it only makes people reluctant to play with me, so I decided to work on accepting loss and learning from it. I wish I could say this is an easy task, but it was not. I'm much more relaxed about losing a game at this point in my life. I am learning that losing at anything is not a statement about my very being. It does not determine my worth as a human being. The rage is gone. It has taken me a good deal of time, but I decided that winning a game is not all it's cracked up to be. A game is just a game, nothing more. I still prefer winning.

ESCAPE

Often depressed and despairing,

My world has changed.

Desiring to escape my folly,

I storm the citadel of freedom. (1954)

I believed I made the best of a bad situation, but resigned myself to being lonely. I am considered a friendly person who has friends and makes friends easily, however, I seldom open myself up to be vulnerable in a relationship. The person I present to the world probably looks as normal as can be. What I feel inside is a different world. One of the issues that continues to plague me to this day is a feeling that I am something of a stranger in a strange land. It is as though I am an alien in the most extreme way: I've fallen in from space, from a far-off galaxy. As a small child I often felt like a part of me had been left in another world and that if I let my foot dangle over the side of the bed, someone from that other world would pull me back there. I had very little knowledge about this other world, but I did know that it terrified me. When I mentioned this world to Mama, she told me not to think about it.

I usually feel as though I have nothing in common with those around me, that we speak different languages, and, at times, I fail to comprehend even the most blatant social cues. Part of my problem stems from the radical shift of languages and cultures I have been experiencing throughout my life. When I see myself, I see a person who stands out from the crowd when I would like to blend in. I am so set on sounding and looking like an average person that I even keep beautiful fantasies and thoughts to myself. So, I present the person I believe the world will accept, not the person I experience inside. I seldom give others a chance to accept ME, the person under the mask.

THOUGHTS

I sit

And ponder

My predicament.

My state of being:

Anemic relationships,

Black, empty days,

Terrifying sleepless nights,

Unconnected world.

Who am I?

Destined to be alone? (1954)

Living at the camp was difficult as my father continued to drink excessively. He managed to once more find a place where to socialize with others meant to drink to excess. When not drinking at home, he went to a bar in Wallaceburg or Mitchell's Bay. Sometimes Mom would ask Corrie and me to go along with Dad in the hope that he might come home sooner. We would have to wait in the car. The bars had men's sides and women's sides, as men and

123

women couldn't drink together unless they came to the bar as a couple. You know, the blue laws. Once, I got so angry and tired of waiting that I went into the men's side to get him. He was very angry with this bold behavior on my part.

"Don't you know that girls are not allowed here?" he said.

I replied, "How could we get you out of here if we can't come and get you? We want to go home."

He was furious with my question. He failed to comprehend that Corrie and I just were not happy to continue sitting in the car waiting. We had already waited two hours. I could never understand the appeal of alcohol. Alcoholism tends to be genetic, and, sad to say, Ria became an alcoholic and drug user in her adult life. Corrie and I have always been cautious when it comes to drinking.

My father got into trouble with the Royal Canadian Mounted Police because he tried to smuggle beer and cigarettes from the United States. We came home from school to find the camp overrun with Provincial Police and Mounties.

A tall, burly Mountie spoke up first, "We are going to search your entire camp as we have evidence that you have been smuggling cigarettes and alcohol. Here is our warrant."

They were searching the entire camp. We were terrified to see the police at our home.

After several hours, the same Mountie came to us and spoke loudly: "Mr. Huige, we will be taking you with us as we have found a considerable amount of contraband. You will be facing a judge."

It was frightening to see all of this happen. I wondered how we would survive without Dad. On the other hand, I was secretly glad and I would not even mind if they kept him. Mom said we would be okay, but we weren't so sure. She turned out to be right, though; I think he got a big fine for this but nothing else. At least, that was all we were aware of. This is another issue we never spoke about as a family.

I think that he learned nothing from this experience. He continued to believe that his drinking was not a problem and we were making up tales about his behavior when drunk. When drunk, he almost always closed the day with violent outbursts such as smashing the dinner on the floor, yelling about something he thought was a slight, or hitting one of us. Mom said very little when he destroyed the dinner she had prepared, however she did look very angry. I had no idea how Mom dealt with Dad. I think she must have been convincing herself to look past his episodes of drinking and rage, and decided complaining did no good. I found out later from Corrie that Mom told Dad that if he ever did this again (smashing dinner on the floor) that she would leave him. I had thought she was in the middle of her own battle with depression and didn't have the energy to confront his behavior. I was surprised she had given him an ultimatum, although he did repeat the tantrums and she did not leave him.

We three children worked before and after school and all day during vacation. We made some money when we cleaned fish or sold worms to fishermen. Dad often offered our services for free, but most people thought it was only fair to pay us something for our work. I remember feeling exhausted a good deal of the time. I wondered how long this lifestyle would last. Putting one foot in front of the other and making it through the day was getting very tiresome. This was not a great life for any kid.

One day, when things were feeling particularly intolerable, we were told that Dad had sold the camp. We cheered this move, as we saw a bleak future for us in our present lifestyle. While we were happy that we were, hopefully, moving back to a more normal life, we were also aware that we would miss some of the friends we made at the high school. We would have to start over again in a new school and a new neighborhood. I felt as though I would perpetually be "the new kid." Going through the "new" routine again was something I was not looking forward to. I was, however, thrilled to be leaving "country living" and hopeful that our next home would be more like the homes of other kids my age. I was envisioning a home where Dad went to work, Mom had more time for us and our house, and the kids would go to school. Most important of all, I prayed that Dad would stop drinking alcohol.

Once more we were surprised as we had no input in this change. We were told that since we were American citizens, we could only stay in Canada for five years or lose our American citizenship. As an adult, I believed that this move was possibly the result of Dad's problem with the Mounties, and that we lost our visa to live in Canada because he had broken the law, so we had to move to the United States. I don't know if this is true, but it is a striking coincidence that within months of his trouble with the Mounties, we sold the camp and were moving back to the United States. Dad was not well and was definitely drinking too much. He had diabetes and it was once more out of control. Again, the thought was that a move would solve things.

We never had any warning about dramatic changes in our lives, such as major moves, until after the decisions had been made. There was not even a buildup of tension to give us some idea that something was about to happen. Once more, I knew nothing. Having my world turned upside down repeatedly enhanced my feelings of impotence. I felt at the mercy of Mom and Dad, who seemed incapable of taking the whole family into account. I also saw Dad as impulsive and driven by what he wanted at the moment. There seemed to be very little planning for the future and no thought of what would be best for the family. We asked ourselves: "Where do we go now? What happens to us? What kind of work will Dad do? What does Mom think about this?" We all had opinions but kept them to ourselves. Once more we packed our belongings with no idea where we were going. As I looked around the house I knew that I would not miss the porch/bedroom I had shared with my sisters. Maybe we would have heat in our next home. Maybe we would have a regular house. Maybe we would have neighbors we would have something in common with. Maybe our next school would be challenging and we could get involved in activities, even those held in the evenings. I was looking forward to what could be wonderful changes for us. I was really ready to go.

BACK IN THE USA 1955-1958

We bought a home in Grosse Pointe Farms. It was a real house, not large, but definitely more comfortable and bigger than anything we had lived in since leaving Europe. The home was beautiful, with a wonderful front porch and a large picture window in the living room. It even had two bathrooms and four bedrooms and you can bet we were happy about that. We also had a wonderful backyard. It wasn't as big as the yard we had in Europe, but it was a private backyard we could enjoy. It was on an ordinary street with homes of a similar size and value. I enjoyed making this house our own. I painted the inside and did my share of repairing the plaster. We loved having great neighbors and we didn't feel as alone as we had felt in Canada. Life was looking up for us. In September, Corrie and I started at Grosse Pointe High School. I was in the tenth grade and Corrie was in the ninth grade. Ria had decided to remain in Canada and attend a boarding school in Chatham. This decision on Ria's part was a big surprise for me. I never dreamed that she wanted boarding school. I think she thought that since she had begun her High School years in the Canadian system and she was in her last year, it made sense for her to finish in this system. Hence…boarding school. I think she also wanted to get away from home as things weren't looking any better for us.

The difference between the two educational systems was shocking and wonderful. We were finally being challenged and I loved experiencing classes where I had to do some work. The school was elegant and had a number of different buildings. Everything was first class. The library was fantastic. The rooms were spacious, the class size was smaller, and there was marble all over the place. The kids played an incredible number of sports, many of which I had never even seen played. We even had a swimming pool and everyone had to take swimming lessons. I loved the idea, but I had never changed my clothes anywhere except in my own room at home. I was so embarrassed and tried to wait until everyone was gone, but then a new class entered the changing area and I was now late for class and again exposed in front of everyone. No one really paid any attention, but this was definitely a challenge for me. The school was very close to Lake St. Clair, and the campus was an amazingly beautiful site. I couldn't believe that I had the privilege of attending this spectacular learning institution.

Corrie and I were faced with a totally different learning experience. We went from an easy learning environment to a very challenging one. My earlier math experiences had been limited, and I never really recovered. Higher math always proved a challenge for me because my introduction had been so poor. In Canada, elementary math had only simple adding and subtracting and nothing more complicated. There was no pre-algebra. Geometry was the ninth grade math and algebra was tenth grade. It was exactly the opposite in the United States. However, I loved the fact that we were now in challenging classes with classmates who could also keep us on our toes. English, history, and biology were my favorite classes. In spite of my crazy education, I did very well at Grosse Pointe High School.

Corrie has always felt that I was the smart one and she was not. She probably got this from Mom, who frequently declared that I was the smart one and Corrie was the pretty one. It's silly to think that you could only be one or the other. At least, neither of us thought that being both pretty and smart was an option. I was not aware that Corrie had taken up this attribution as thoroughly as she did. She struggled in this new learning experience. As for me, I always felt like the ugly duckling of the family. It seemed I took the attribution concerning appearance quite directly. As adults, we've had a chance to talk about these things and share feelings. We have also had time to make some new decisions which are not based on attributions others made about us. I have been able to look at photos and actually find myself to have been somewhat attractive. I still can't say that I was as pretty as Corrie.

It was now 1956, and as school progressed, we got involved in more and more activities and both of us had jobs as well. Corrie was involved in tennis and other athletics and I was in the A Capella Choir, photography, and other activities. To be a part of the choir, you had to know how to read music. I never had a music lesson, so reading music was not part of my skill set. I was fortunate in that I only needed to hear a tune once to repeat it fairly accurately. I don't know if Mr. Finch, the director, was aware I just had the music memorized, but he did not kick me out. I have been in choirs all of my life, including in my old age, and have picked up more and more skills at music, but I still cannot really read music beyond knowing when to go up the scale or when to go down. Singing as a tenor continues to be one of my favorite activities and provides me with a chance to feel a part of a very special community. Choirs became family for me and continue to be so.

Our part-time jobs also became integral parts of our schedules. I worked twenty hours a week as a soda jerk for Sanders at 75 cents per hour, and Corrie worked for a dentist. I was grateful that I had very little time to dwell on my inner thoughts. I was having difficulty hanging onto what was real in my world. My family life was disastrous. As a sign that learning from experience was not my Dad's forte, he bought another bar, but he was too sick to work there.

I WAS FURIOUS AT MOM for letting this happen. Why didn't she put her foot down and stop this craziness? As soon as I said this, Mom began to cry, and there was no talking about this issue. If I had given this much thought, I would have realized that Mom knew she needed to support us financially. She understood the bar business and had not worked in any other capacity in this country. She chose what she knew she could do. Starting a new occupation was probably more than she could have handled at this stage of her life. I wish I had been able to look at life from Mom's vantage point; I would have been easier on her and complained less. Mom, who still did not drive, had to take the bus to this bar which was in an unsavory part of Detroit. Once we got our driver's licenses, Corrie and I would often drive her to and from work, but she still would occasionally return by bus in the middle of the night. We were really worried about her safety.

In the meantime, Ria had remained in Canada, and then joined us in the United States. She had an unfortunate affair which ended badly. She was quite depressed and had no focus in her life. Mom and Dad had been invited to the wedding of the son of Dad's childhood friend and Ria joined them on the trip to the Canadian Niagara area just to get out of the house. She met Leonard at the wedding and fell in love. Within months, they were married and began a family. She had been in and out of the house for years and was ready to leave home permanently and start a family in St. Catherines, Ontario. She became a Canadian citizen and felt happy with this decision. Within a year, she had her first child.

Dad was sick and getting sicker by the day. It was much more than his diabetes. He was bleeding profusely from his anus and also had a multitude of digestive issues. The doctors could not give us a diagnosis. He was unable to work and could hardly walk.

Mom was exhausted but kept up the charade that all was fine. None of us talked about the many issues facing the family. I could tell that Mom was depressed and stressed. She was worried about Dad's health, but she kept her worries to herself.

Occasionally, I saw her crying.

I would ask, "How can I help?" and her answer was usually, "I'm fine. Don't worry." She continued doing the bookkeeping for the bar and much of the actual bartending. I tried to help her, but had no idea what to do. I did not offer to tend the bar, but I did increase what I did around the house and looked after Dad more as he needed more help. Mom often told me, "I'm just being silly," when I tried to talk to her or help. She had not been able to speak her mind or share her feelings with anyone since we left Europe. We were her only support system and we did not do a very good job at this. She was generally adapting to what she believed people wanted to hear. She was very different from the Mama I knew in Belgium. But despite all the work and all the complications in her life, she never gave up. She put one foot in front of the other and continued to work. She never complained. She was still my hero.

School and learning continued to be a respite for me. I loved reading, talking about the books I had read, talking politics with friends, and all types of artistic endeavors. I knew that the only road I wanted to travel was to the university. I was very successful in high school and was accepted at various universities. Dad, however, was vehemently against my attending college.

"Women can be secretaries or housewives, but university is wasted on them. Look, Ria got married and she's starting a family; you should do the same." This was his mantra. I was furious.

I screamed back, "I want to go to college; I want to be more than a secretary or a housewife. I have skills and I'm a very good student."

I stood my ground but applied only to Wayne State University as Dad was so ill I was afraid to move any distance away. I knew that Mom needed me to look after Dad. I was fully aware that I still wanted to look after Dad and at this school, I could live at home and be a caretaker. Very little was said at home of my transgression. (going to university) This was probably the first time I strongly defied Dad, and I breathed a sigh of relief that I was still alive. Mom was quietly supportive and stated she was happy I had not chosen to settle for a career I did not want. I was grateful for her support.

ESCAPE TO THE UNIVERSITY - 1958-1962

I rode the bus daily to the university. It was about an hour's trip through what several of my friends described as some of the worst sections of Detroit. This was my first introduction to racial issues that were growing increasingly more virulent in the city. Many of the homes were sad examples of the abuse people heaped on their environment. It was also clear to me that many of the people who lived in the neighborhoods I passed through didn't have the money to pay for upkeep on houses. To me, it looked as though most of the buildings were collapsing. People crowded the streets, and loud shouts filled the air. I was totally naive when it came to understanding how other people lived. I didn't even understand how average middle-class Caucasians, such as the members of my family, dealt with the world, and I was totally out of my safety zone when it came to having any understanding of how the average black person lived.

As people crowd into the bus, I feel I am in a different world. Even the smells and language are foreign to me. I am aware that I am afraid. However, as I listen to the friendly repartee of the people around me, I gradually find myself relaxing and enjoying the experience of being in a different world. I stop paying attention to the worn clothes and the slang which peppers the conversation and decide this is the beginning of my education. 1958

I chose to major in English honors and history with a minor in French. My classes were wonderful and I even managed to make some friends. We spent time together talking about our goals and our lives as we sat in the student center and shared a meal. I was already having new and pleasurable experiences. Although I eagerly launched myself into my new life, anxiety continued to plague me. Would my new friends discover that I was really a fraud? Was I good enough? When will the next disaster strike?

I sailed through the classes, perpetually on the dean's list. I continued to work several jobs. I got a job at the university as a secretary, but had no idea how to type, and typing was one of the requirements for the position. The winter that year was very cold, and some of the houses owned by the university on the campus were old and not well heated or insulated. When my boss complained about how slowly I was typing, I replied: "If you only heated the place, perhaps my frozen fingers would be able to work to your satisfaction."

The person I said this to was a professor who always had a smart-ass or sarcastic question or comment, so he loved this kind of response. In the past, he always seemed to be firing student employees, but he kept me for more than two years, until I left after graduation.

In response to my statement, he said: "Well then, I assume that the typing will improve in the spring?" I said "yes" and worked feverishly to meet this goal. I taught myself how to type and the job was wonderful.

While focusing on our studies, Corrie and I continued to look after Dad, as his ill health had progressed and we found out that he was seriously ill with cancer. At first, there was no diagnosis, and we were somewhat short with him as we had trouble believing the seriousness of what he was dealing with. At some point, we were told that he had colon cancer. This was in the 1950s, and cancer was a dirty word. I didn't share with friends that my father had cancer. I felt shame and fear. There were many myths spread about this disease, including that it was catching. We were somewhat freaked out about this diagnosis. Even though we believed, and were told that cancer was not catching, we were still apprehensive. We did eventually become more comfortable with caring for Dad.

I felt such mixed feelings about Dad. I knew he was ill, but I felt rage towards him. I didn't express any of my feelings directly, but I felt them in my heart. I felt mixed up when it came to both of my parents. I was angry that Mom was still working in the bar and not taking care of Dad, and I felt angry about taking care of him. I was aware that Mom had to work to pay the bills.

Corrie graduated from high school and got a scholarship for nursing school. She moved out of the house…she flew the coop…I felt jealous that she felt free enough to take this step, and break the very strong bond with Mom. I knew that it was painful for her to move on, but she felt a palpable need to separate from the craziness of the past. I stayed home and went to university, but I felt abandoned by my sister. I knew she had to do this, but I did not like it. Mom needed someone and I was "it." I, too, felt a strong need to move away, but in all honesty, I was also terrified of the prospect of facing the world on my own. I saw it as a kind of all-or-nothing proposition. My symbiotic bond with my Mom was much too strong and left very little room to breathe. I felt trapped in spite of this intense bond with Mom. I loved Mom with all my heart, but I felt totally alone. I knew that our relationship was not good for either one of us.

A DEATH IN THE FAMILY

Dad was unable to help Mom at all. He had been ill since we moved from Canada and barely had the energy to get out of bed. He bled profusely from his anus but it was still many months before he was diagnosed with colon cancer. His cancer was stage four. He finally had his colon removed and was trying to live with a colostomy bag. He was a failure when it came to looking after himself. He couldn't stand, and he couldn't look at his stoma. This once powerful man was a shadow of his former self. Mom worked very long hours and did not have much time to help in Dad's care. He never adjusted to the colostomy. After the operation, he could only defecate in a bag, which needed to be changed when he pooped. He never learned how to clean himself up and put a new bag on. He was in agony a good deal of the time. Pain medication provided little relief. He could barely walk. Although I remained angry with him, I looked after him. He did not deserve all of this pain. I prayed that God would relieve him of this pain. I prayed to God to be a kinder soul, to be relieved of my anger. I struggled with myself, hoping that I could find a softer, kinder me. I wanted to love him and care for him, but my anger stood between us.

Corrie and I took care of Dad during the last few years of his life. When Corrie was away at nursing school, his care was my responsibility. This caretaking was very difficult. He was in so much pain and looking after his colostomy was an incredibly intimate and, I feel ashamed to admit, disgusting task. His stoma was often very tender and bloody. We wondered if it was infected but got very little clarification from the medical community. His doctors were not good at talking to family and explaining what was going on. They spoke more to Corrie because, as a nursing student, they saw her as part of the medical community. The hardest part for me was the intense intimacy of this care. I had never seen a naked man before, and it was very difficult for me to touch Dad in private places, but in order to clean him, I had to do so. I had never had any physical intimacy, including hugs or kisses, so this was something very new for me to acclimate to. It was also hard for Dad. He started out embarrassed, frustrated, and angry but grew to gradually accept what was happening to his body. He slowly learned to accept help. I slowly learned to be helpful. I became aware of what he needed and what he would accept in the form of help. I also learned to keep my embarrassment from impeding my task at hand. I had to put my feelings away and focus on Dad. I needed to be sensitive to Dad's embarrassment and how I could help minimize these feelings on all of our parts. Corrie seemed to be more comfortable with the physical parts of Dad's care. While Corrie and I worked together helping Dad, we did not share our feelings about this. We slowly learned how to talk to him and in some ways, we both got to know our father.

I knew that someone had to take care of Dad, and I decided to give in and do so. Initially, my resolve to look after him was not the action of a loving heart. As time progressed, and I related to Dad more and more, my caretaking did become the action of a loving heart. I learned to actually have conversations with him and stopped worrying about whether or not he would approve of what I had to say. I remember a wonderful conversation we had about strawberries. We talked about how we liked to eat them…with sugar or without…on pancakes or ice cream. We reminisced about squishing them with our forks and how good they tasted on toast. We learned to laugh together.

All of this happened within three years of leaving Canada. It was almost as though we were finally beginning to move into a life that was somewhat normal and then we were hit with another major problem. I had many discussions with God about the unfairness of the trials he was putting my family through. Why were all of these tragedies visited on my family? I thought it would help us if we could talk to one another about our feelings, but we kept our feelings and thoughts to ourselves. Ours was a silent yet busy home punctuated by occasional violent outbursts, but the violence had decreased as Dad's condition became more critical.

Caretaking for Dad was complicated by the fact that I was so angry with him for the years of abuse. He had been cruel and mean to me, and the last thing I wanted was to look after him in such an intimate fashion. As time progressed, what did happen was that I probably came face to face with the man Mom married. He was not drinking now, and I could have real conversations with him. We spoke about his rage and the difficulty he had adjusting to children from the moment he entered our lives. He said he was sorry he treated us the way he did. He really did want us in his life. And the drink…the drink…He asked for forgiveness for his drunken behavior. He was so weak and sick, but he talked, and he wanted to talk. Even though I struggled against feeling more positive about Dad, I got to know him as a totally different person. I got to see him at his most vulnerable. I heard what he said, and after struggling with myself, I can even say that I came to love him. Maybe my discussions with God did pay off. He didn't take the problem away, but it certainly was becoming more manageable.

While I was sitting by his bedside, we spoke about our lives together. We talked and talked. We talked about important issues, such as looking after Mom, and we talked about little things, such as his love of strawberries. These painful times were precious to me. He died when I was twenty. I had gotten to know him in the last year of his life after having lived with all the conflict he instilled in our relationship since he came into my life when I was seven years old. It was almost as though living those last years in agony while we nursed him gave us all the opportunity to make amends. I was able to ask him to forgive me for my anger at him and he was able to ask for forgiveness. He accepted me for the person I had become. He even accepted my decision to attend university.

The last month of his life was spent in the hospital, and Corrie, who was in nursing school but had taken a leave of absence, acted as a private nurse for him. We split the time looking after him. He was not left alone. She reported that she had long, meaningful conversations with Dad and felt heard and loved by him. We mourned in our own ways. He died quietly, and, I think, at peace with his family and himself. The funeral was sad for all of us. I thought of what I had missed in all of those years of conflict. I was burying a man I had just gotten to know. I cried for my loss. I was still so conflicted, but life went on: Corrie returned to nursing school and I continued my work at the university. Mom continued to run the bar.

Our lives are now quite separate. With Dad's death, I think I will be released from my torment. I am not. My despair increases and so do my nightmares. Once more, we do not speak to one another of our loss. I am, however, very surprised that I cried deeply at his funeral. What am I grieving about? This was someone I hated, feared, and loved. I mourn what was missing in our life together. I would never have the father I yearn for.1960

FATHER

All absorbing blackness,

The domain of night.

I lose my being

In your depths.

You devour all my identities.

And I am left

A petrified, hollow shell.

At last,

Perceptual adaptation,

And degrees of blackness appear.

Some light from somewhere.

It should bring comfort.

As I again

Partially become.

But no -

Shadows appear.

Not welcome, familiar tangibles

Or objects on which

To ground my world.

Rather - another world appears.

I see my father

Rising from the grave-

Pale, emaciated,

A death camp victim.

He shuffles forward.

Menacing-

With furious hollows

Which once held tempestuous eyes.

He shuffles forward,

Hunched over

As though still in pain.

Shorter than in life,

But stronger.

"Die too," he says.

"But they'll bury me!

Lock me in some minute space,

And I'll decay completely.

It won't be just a fleeting thought

It won't be this unseen inner decay.

I'll rot and turn to dust."

He laughs,

And laughter penetrates my soul

The monster is real and attacks.

Awakened by screams, they come

Hear the absurd tale

And laugh. "You're crazy!

And laugh some more. (1960)

Although my conscious mind had learned to love a different father, the being inhabiting my dream world felt somewhat at odds with this new image. In one sense, I felt an enormous relief after Dad died. With this relief came guilt and a sense that no one should feel better or even happy that someone has died. I was grateful that he was no longer suffering, but I knew that this was not the only reason for my relief. I saw my main problem as gone…he could no longer torture me. I no longer had to deal with the complexities of a painful relationship. I didn't have to hear breaking dishes and rage-filled screaming. However, I also had to deal with the knowledge that I would never experience the love of a father I had fantasized about. He would never tell me that he was proud of me. This awareness was very hard to swallow. It was almost as though I had to choose which father would be the greatest influence on my future. I chose the father of the last two years as he was someone I could actually have a conversation with. This was easier said than done, and I found myself listening to a confusing mess, the alcoholic, rageful parent and the sick, confused, and kind parent. My thoughts about my father continue to have a painful influence on decisions and relationships even into the present day.

Veils drop one by one.

Can the veiled sister still pray?

Will the earthquake and tremble?

Will those who see...run for life?

By the temple, she will pray…

That her past will not betray her.

Perhaps these veils hide new life…

And mysteries she fears bring light. (1960)

In writing this memoir, I asked Corrie how she dealt with Dad's death. When she went back to nursing school, Corrie said that every time there was a code on the floor, she rushed to it and felt compelled to be there as the person died. She did this for about a year and then, one day, while in chapel praying, she heard Dad say that she could stop rushing to the codes and that he was fine now. She was able to stop this compulsion. When I asked Ria how she dealt with Dad's death, she said she didn't really have a problem. She felt resolved and didn't really understand why Corrie and I had so much conflict when it came to relating to Dad. I couldn't believe what she said. I still find it sad that we did not talk about Dad's death or even share our feelings. We had continued to abide by the code of silence when

144

it came to feelings or even uncomfortable experiences. Staying locked up within oneself takes its toll. It breeds increased isolation, repetitive negative thoughts, and frequent nightmares. Occasionally, Corrie and I sought out some help. I found a therapist but my lack of trust continued to be a major roadblock for me. I talked about some safe issues but kept my feelings to myself. My strength was still my ability to perform and I believed I fooled everyone into concluding that all was well with me.

LIFE AFTER DAD

At this point, I was twenty years old. Writing about my life and living my life is increasingly difficult, as I am slowly moving toward crashing and burning emotionally. At some level, I knew that the emotional burden I was carrying was overwhelming. I was on the verge of leaving home, but although I desperately wanted to leave, I was also terrified of being on my own. Looking after Dad while he was dying provided an excuse for staying at home, and after his death, looking after Mom was a good reason and an excuse. I found it excruciating to deal with my feelings and somehow, I decided that my problems were physical in nature. I had stomach aches, headaches, and nightmares. One day, while I was returning home from the pharmacy, a car jumped the center island on Mack Avenue and hit my car head-on. It was a drunk driver. I broke my neck and injured my jaw. I was terrified. I could have died and my fear was that I would be with Dad. Another part of me experienced this accident as a reprieve from my inner conflict. I had something else to dwell on. I also felt that the injuries I suffered were punishment for the myriad of hostile feelings possessing my psyche. If this was punishment, maybe I could let up on myself and give myself time to ease up on negative thinking.

Injuries suffered in the accident resulted in a cervical spinal fusion and jaw surgery which confined me to a hospital for several months. I spent one month confined exclusively to a circle bed. I felt trapped and terribly alone. I was frightened that I might not be able to walk. Corrie was not around and Mom couldn't come to see me as she was working. I told none of my school friends as I felt ashamed that I was as helpless as I was. I felt so alone and abandoned. Once out of the circle bed, where the only exercise I got was to be turned several times a day, I felt enormous relief. It was, however, extremely painful to once more be on my feet. I felt so alone in dealing with this injury. Rehab was not an easy experience. I could deal with the physical pain, but the psychological fears, embedded in needing help with almost everything I had to do for myself, were almost intolerable. I worked on rehabilitation as though there was no tomorrow. It's ironic that while I craved love and wanted to be looked after, I also detested my needy self. I made sure that I did not miss any of my assignments from school and as crazy as it sounds, I continued to excel as a student. I was grateful that I could still walk and do all I needed to do. For six months, I had to wear a heavy metal cervical support mechanism to protect my neck. The physical pain I experienced felt like a relief and a respite from the pain in my heart and soul. With pain, I knew I was alive. I could focus on the pain and not the craziness in my mind. Dealing with reality and the past was something I was not ready to do. I felt locked in the pain of all of my past experiences. I began to express my psychological pain as physical. I needed to find some way to release the negative energy that possessed me. Poetry continued to provide some solace, and a place to express my pain.

GREMLINS

Neophyte

Confused by myriads of emotions

Unable to escape.

The gremlins of the world attack,

Oh Shamans

Where are those great curative powers

To resuscitate this dying spirit.

Cryptic aberrations

That strange translucence

Damn the mutability

Which fails to provide a moment's respite.

Again phlegmatic responses

To nebulous stimuli.

After the anger

The curtain of lethargy drops.

Insipid panaceas

Sold by obtuse old men

To eradicate all terror

Prove noxious.

Once more, the predatory horde

Breaks through a weakened defense

Mutilating,

Spreading venomous platitudes.

Where has it gone

That one small accident

Which was a human life? (1960)

I was depressed and trying to hold my life together. Despite my psychological decline, I continued to be on the dean's list and to work for the university. It was vitally important to me that I maintained my grade point average. I loved my classes and found them to be very much like the garden of my early years. However, I was questioning everything. I became more involved with religion, joining the National Newman Federation, a group for Roman Catholic students, and Wayne State's Newman Club. I immersed myself in religion, hoping to find some solace, some answers as to why bad things had happened to me and my family. I found some friends and worked on understanding the belief system I had grown up in. I loved both the spiritual and the social experiences which were part of the Newman Club. In fact, I even became a national officer. I had friends and found myself able to influence others. In spite of this success and support, I slowly continued my slide into a maelstrom of feelings I did not understand. God and religion did not provide what I needed. I had not managed to run away from my past. I could not find myself. I was lost. In writing about this time in my life, I'm aware that I have no idea as to the time frame many of these experiences fit. I was confused and lost.

Everything seems like a blur and I feel as though I'm running marathon after marathon. I can barely breathe. Details escape me. I'm running for my life. I can no longer decide between safe and unsafe worlds; everywhere seems unsafe. I worry about my sanity. What is happening to me? Can I go on this way? 1961

I had believed that my father was my main problem; he was now dead, and my pain seemed to have gotten worse. I felt so incredibly confused. I knew I needed help. I once more entered psychotherapy. Again it was a typical one-on-one approach, very little direct feedback, and a great deal of silence. The silence drove me nuts. It terrified me. I was back in the bomb shelter, waiting to die. I felt smothered by it. I felt wordless anger interspersed with terror. It puzzled me that when confronted with silence, my usually highly verbal self could think of nothing. My mind was blank. I had nothing available to say. The more blank my mind was, the higher my anxiety level grew. Therapy was not helping me. I felt frozen and empty.

I'm searching for some answers to past feelings and behaviors, some of which still torment me. I keep wondering why I am spending years spinning my wheels in my own shit. What did I find in crazy behavior and sadness that must have gratified me enough to continue aberrant behaviors for such a long time? My early years were replete with high-energy excitement and drama, and with such intense feelings that I knew I was alive. When I numbed myself in order to stop my feelings, I was not sure what being alive felt like. When life was moving at a normal pace, I was bored. I wanted more energy. So, I was motivated to keep the intensity going. I wasted so much precious time. Perhaps the drama included in hysteria continues the pathology and actually becomes addictive. Being a psychological mess might also provide internal excuses in the event I failed to excel at something. Despite feeling crazy, I continued to perform well but felt alone. For some reason, I did not savor the accolades of the world around me. It was not enough. However, suddenly, a change took place in my thinking.

And when I think of you,

My friend,

A new world is found,

Rising from ashes of past holocausts

Fresh hope for a new life. (1961)

When I was twenty-one, I fell in love and wow...what a jolt. Suddenly, all of my problems seemed to disappear and I was not alone. Michael was an Irish intern working at a local hospital. He was in Grosse Pointe with seventeen friends, all interns, for the summer. He was a very handsome redhead and also very bright. Our conversations were wonderful and it was delightful to find someone I could converse with on all kinds of topics. We spent a lot of time together on the beach, running our toes through the warm, sunbaked sand. I felt like a carefree child. I didn't feel the need to worry about classes or jobs; my focus was on Michael and our relationship. I felt high and my energy felt boundless. I was on the "top of the world." The relationship felt intellectually and emotionally intense, but it remained chaste.

We had a lot of fun and did some outrageous things. We even took a wild trip with six friends to St. Catherine and visited Ria's family. While on this trip, we invited ourselves onto a ship entering the Welland Canal and enjoyed an evening drinking, singing, and dancing with the crew. The whole experience left me feeling wonderfully high and I hoped we could continue this relationship long distance. I thought that maybe I could escape the terrors which had possessed my life experience before Michael. I believed that I truly loved Michael. He had clearly told me that he planned on going back to Ireland at the end of the summer. He returned to Ireland and I never heard from him again. I felt a deep sadness. I felt that maybe I had fooled myself into believing that my feelings had been reciprocated. I tried to blame Michael for my hurt and initially convinced myself that I should not have trusted him. In retrospect, my feelings were so intense that I probably frightened him. I'm aware that I was not an easy person to talk with at the end of this relationship. I was crushed. A short experience with love was not my cure. I was back where I started. I think that on some level, I was trying to prove that relationships could only end badly for me…that there was something wrong with me I was not loveable.

Merlin's rod swung wide,

The spell was cast,

Our minds met

And it felt good and warm.

So long a wait

So brief a moment.

Did you know this moment's cost?

Could you feel my rising fears?

I wondered all the while -

Would you, too, desert me? (1961)

That love was not to be, and I returned to indulging depressive thoughts. Instead of using this experience as proof that I could be loved, I used it as proof that I was not loveable.

I did have choices. I continued searching for meaning in my life. Could I find another love? Was I lovable? Was my life to be loveless? Did I even want to let myself be vulnerable again? Did I want to take another chance? I knew that this was just one experience and that I was young and had my whole life ahead of me, but I really built this up to be monumental. The experience led to an all-or-nothing decision: "If this doesn't work, then no relationship will work for me." I felt rejected and ashamed. The shame involved wondering what was wrong with me or was the rejection caused by something I had done. I overlooked the fact that Michael had been clear that he was only there for the summer. That was it. It had nothing to do with me or anything I had done.

Michael was my only love. I wrote to him, but got no response. I don't know the specific decisions I made after this love failed, but I was apparently bent on going through life alone. I no longer trusted my feelings and certainly did not want to experience the sharp pain of loss again; however, I do not believe this experience was the sole cause of my decision to remain alone. I believe I had actually been terrified of closeness for most of my life. I had dreams of having a family, but they never included a husband. I find it interesting that I never allowed myself another intimate relationship. In fact, the thought of intimacy frightened and even repulsed me. I have many wonderful friendships which I treasure; however, I never married. I even had several very nice men ask me out but I rejected them, although I have no rational reason why I did so.

I moved on with work and classes. It was full speed ahead. No looking back. I tried to shake off the depression I was experiencing. I pushed myself harder. I knew there must be a way out of my black mood, but I had no idea where it might be. I had a fleeting thought that I might need to take a look at my wartime experiences, but I talked myself out of this. The last thing I wanted to do was go there.

LOOKING FOR HOME

I graduated from Wayne State University in 1962. I did not go to my graduation; no one from my family went or encouraged me to go and I did not ask them. It was no big deal. I decided to return to where I believed I had been happy: Belgium. In some strange way, I decided that my life in war-torn Europe had been so much happier than my experiences in the United States or Canada. I had been enveloped by a loving family. We played together and laughed together. We held each other at times of terror and most important of all, we were never alone. At least, it felt that way to me. I was going to study at the University of Louvain and at the Sorbonne. I was convinced that I could recapture the old feelings of security and love I had left behind. I was sure that I would feel that I truly belonged in Europe. I had never felt that I belonged in either the United States or Canada. I felt I looked different; my name was foreign, my clothes were strange and not like my friends', and I spoke, somehow, a different language. Now, I would truly be back in the land where I belonged. Nothing made sense to me, but I believed "going back home" would set the world right again.

Unblemished

Laughing child

With golden curls

Yes, there was a time

In another land

Far different from this world

Where singing, dancing, love….

Encompassed all. (1955)

I packed pretty much everything I had and boarded a boat to the world I idealized. The boat trip took ten days and the seas were rough, as they had been on the trip to America. I was excited about the certainty that I would find myself again. I had myself convinced that all would be well; the people I loved and who loved me would once more be there for me, as they had been when I was a child. I knew that my immediate family would not be there, but I dismissed the significance of that fact.

I remembered my first Atlantic trip. The boat was quite similar. It was basically a steel tub with a lot of metal and wooden stairs and small staterooms. The seas were again very rough, and I was once more looking for ways to amuse myself. However, I was now an adult and I joined in on the fun in the bar. I connected with a young Dutch engineer. He was a lovely man; however, his face was somewhat disfigured and I was not grown up enough to look past his appearance. We had a wonderful ten days and he came to Oom

Adri's house and asked me out. I was shocked. I had thought we would have a wonderful friendship on the boat and then we would both go our merry ways and never see each other again. I was ready for that, not for a dating relationship. At this point, and I still have no idea why, I told him I did not want to go out. I had really enjoyed my time with him on the boat. I actually think I was frightened about getting involved in another relationship, thinking about my experience with Michael.

When I came to Oom Adri's house, I realized that even though he was my uncle, I had only met him once and I didn't know him or his family. He had come to Dad's funeral, and had been very kind, but I did not know him.

Oom Adri and Tante Loukie had a lovely home and invited me to stay. I did not know any of the family he introduced me to and no one knew me. Again, I felt completely alone, although I was surrounded by family. My head was spinning and I felt totally disconnected from reality. I told myself that I had no expectations, but I knew this was a lie. I wanted to be the child who was an integral part of her family…wherever they might be. I wanted the world to go back in time and reproduce for me the idyllic wartime world I remembered, where I was part of a large family that looked after me. It even sounds strange to me to speak of an "idyllic wartime world." I was so close to this perfect family that I could block out the war itself. I was running and running hard. I wanted to escape the world I lived in, but did the world I wanted to run to actually exist? Once more, I felt like a stranger in a strange land.

Oom Adri was wonderful and his family was very accepting of this stranger in their home; however, they spoke mainly Dutch with a little bit of English scattered in their communications. I was shocked at how poorly I spoke Dutch or Flemish. I could still understand what people said to me in Dutch, but I was back trying to frame a response translating from Dutch to English back to Dutch. I was ashamed that I had forgotten the language I had grown up with. Here I was, again, not able to speak the language of those around me. It never crossed my mind that I had forgotten Flemish. I thought it would always be with me. Once more, I was the "child" who could not express what she wanted and felt.

Once in Belgium, I felt confused. I was no longer a cute little girl looked after by her Mama. I was a grownup who was on her own. My family in Europe had also grown up while I was away. The people I connected with did not resemble the people I had lived with, and they did not know me as I wanted them to know me. They saw a grown woman. I felt like a child. Everyone had grown or changed. No one's life had stood still. I had not known the Dutch family, and was struggling to get to know them. I did not recognize Belgium or my family in Belgium. They respected me and admired the fact that I was a university graduate. That didn't seem to matter to me. I did not know where to start to reconstruct my family. Was it possible?

My needs felt limitless, but I dared not show any of them to anyone, and I don't believe anyone sensed them. At least, I hoped that no one saw this needy person I had become. For some reason, it continued to be important to me that people remain ignorant of what was going on in my head. I felt ashamed of my thoughts and feelings. I was ashamed of how internally critical I was of the people around me who were being kind and generous. I saw my uncles and their families as quiet people who were raising their children in ways I had no frame of reference for. They seemed to make no demands on them and accepted them unconditionally. The children were teens, but they seemed to have few tasks and were waited on. While part of me yearned for this kind of acceptance, this was very different from the way the American me was raised that it actually frightened and angered me. Unconditional love was something foreign to my nuclear family. We had to work and earn everything we got. Nothing came to us simply because we existed.

The world had not stood still for me. Things were not the way they had been years earlier. I believe I sought familiarity and found none. I was particularly distressed that the Flemish language did not return easily for me. I did much better with French, yet my family spoke Flemish and Dutch. Even language was again a barrier for me. I had wanted the world to stand still. In my mind it was as though nothing should have happened to separate us during the missing fourteen years. I was stuck in a time warp.

I moved into a room in Leuven and was told I could take one shower per week. It was a small room with a sink in one corner, a bed, and a small desk with a chair. It was definitely all that I needed. The floor was slanted and walking from one side to the other felt like being in a funhouse. The people around me seemed friendly, and I knew I had to decide if I would do what I needed to do to make this a good place for me. I knew this, but didn't actually feel that I had the power to decide anything. I felt as though life was just happening around me and that I had no power to interact with whatever this "life" was. I did not take advantage of the goodness around me. I had the opportunity to go to some interesting classes, but after just a few attempts to venture out into the classroom, I chose to stop and basically spent most of my time in my room or wandering around. This was actually the first time that performance in school seemed totally insignificant and I put no energy into learning.

From the start, I saw this as this a different world. I seemed to seek out anything I could complain silently about. The cobblestone streets I used to love in Belgium now were trip-and-slip hazards, and the homes were not the beautiful places I remembered. The houses seemed to have much smaller rooms and awkwardly placed stairways and doors. Nothing resembled the comfortable places of my past. Even the bathrooms seemed small without conveniences and they seemed to smell more. Yet we had few indoor bathrooms in World War II Belgium and we relied a great deal on chamber pots. The kitchens were impossibly tiny with few "modern" appliances. Of course, wartime kitchens had no refrigerators or electric stoves. The word "quaint" no longer was a positive for me. I felt like I became the personification of "the ugly American," who always thought that the things in America were so much better than in Europe. All I can say in my defense is I was young and foolish and very confused. I was looking for any way that I could gain control of my experience. I didn't see the happy families who ate very well and engaged in timeless family activities. I didn't see the ageless and beautiful structures all around me. Belgians love flowers and parks and I was surrounded by them. But they didn't exist for me.

I'm not sure what I wanted to see, but I did know this wasn't the world I left. I had counted on finding myself if I returned to the world where I lost myself. I went to see Marieke and she called me "miss," no pet names from the past. She was happy to see me but not in the way I wanted. I don't even think that I knew how I wanted her to greet me or relate to me. I was so confused. Marieke and her family were kind, but I felt like a stranger. She acted as though I was her employer and not a family member. I would not even let myself know that she had been an employee and not a family member. But I was not her child, no matter how much I wanted this deeper connection.

I am amazed that I had so completely built up the image of Belgium as the place where I had been blissfully happy and where I would find happiness. I had wanted time to stand still. I am further amazed that I remembered the war as a time of family closeness I clung to with such ferocity. Gone was the reality of the horrors I had experienced in the war. I refused to let the bombings and the years of fear inhabit the recesses of my conscious mind. I did not succeed in this venture, as fear and bombings and running away had taken charge of my dreams. Returning to my idealized world brought all of the terror back in full, and I still had no way to deal with the past. I had tried to replace the wartime past with a fantasy of life in a magical, peaceful garden where I was looked after and loved. This denial was shattered as I stepped back into reality. Was I ready for this? I felt that I could not deal with the shock of this awareness.

There seemed to be no culture or world where I could fit in. Where did I belong? What could I do to settle this hunger for what no longer existed? What was I actually looking for? With no time machine available, I had to accept that the world had changed and I had to deal with life as it was now. I was so disappointed…so sad. While gathering my feelings, I became aware that I also felt very angry that the world had changed. When looking at how stressful life had been for us in the United States and Canada, it is in some ways not surprising that I had idealized my life in Europe. At least when I was a small child in Europe, the people around me had been loving and kind, in spite of the war going on in the world. I had to find a way to come to terms with the world as it was at this point in my life.

My return "home" was not what I had hoped for. I remained in Europe for about eight months, attending very few classes and basically spending time wandering around the city and hiding in my room while in Leuven. I went to Paris, thinking that I had to get out of my funk and that this magnificent city would be the place to do so. I stayed with a cousin and his family but in my mind, I continued to be silently critical of everything I experienced. While I was grateful for the roof over my head and for the companionship, I could not appreciate the beauty of the world around me. While wandering around, my internal critic was working overtime. Walking along the Seine, I didn't focus on the beautiful gardens and buildings, but instead, I saw the clochards (tramps) who basked in the sun by the sides of the river. I didn't appreciate the beautiful flowers in the many gardens throughout the city but saw the garbage the tourists left instead. I was so disappointed with myself that I could not make this return homework for me. I was upset with myself for being critical about small things. Nothing was right with the world. The only redeeming feature I felt content with was that I kept my feelings and experiences to myself. I don't know if this was truly the case, but I hoped it was so. It is odd that I felt gratified that I didn't seek help. I'm happy that I know better now.

I need to decide where "home" is at this point in my life. I am reeling. I am incredibly disappointed and confused. America is now my home and I need to stop pining for a world that no longer exists and perhaps never did. My head feels like it is about to explode. I am puzzled that I feel so much anger. It's not clear to me what the rage is about, as no one here in Europe has done anything horrible to me. Growing and changing is not a sin. It is what people need to do. I need to get on with this. 1962

WHERE IS HOME

It was now 1963 I had returned to the United States defeated. I decided I needed to plunge into life…maybe that would help my depression. I needed to devise a plan for my life…goals. Direction…where was I going and how would I get there? I loved literature, and what better place to go than to something I loved? I was accepted into a master's program at the University of Michigan in comparative literature and even got a teaching fellowship to pay for it. It never ceases to amaze me that my plans moved ahead so easily. I had no concern that I would not get accepted to the Master's program and I believed I would receive the fellowship which would pay my way. I don't think I fully appreciated this. I also did not fully appreciate that I had the skills to do this job. I should have been thrilled. I just took this accomplishment in stride. Nothing special. I had a room in Ann Arbor which I shared with a friend. Most of the time, I returned home to Grosse Pointe, ostensibly to keep an eye on Mom. I don't know if she needed me or if I needed her.

I loved my classes and learned that I had some skills in psychological interpretations of literature. I published a long article on Gerard de Nerval, focusing on art and schizophrenia in a very reputable publication known as *American Imago.* As I plunged into the study of psychopathology, what I did discover was that the more that I learned about psychology, the more I realized that I needed some help. I was self-destructive, suicidal, and morbidly depressed. When I was in school or at work, I seemed to "turn myself on," and I would become energetic and even interesting. At other times, I stumbled through my days in a haze. I don't know how I made it from day to day. I knew I needed help. I had seen a therapist in the past, and I finally started seeing a psychotherapist again, but still resisted letting anyone in. I played games with the therapist, couldn't stand any silent moments, and tried to suppress the myriad of emotions which felt so very foreign and yet familiar to me. Silence terrified me, and I was once again in an air raid shelter, this time with a war of my own making. I couldn't even bring myself to talk about this. I couldn't get myself to talk for 45 minutes. I didn't feel and I didn't talk. I both wanted and did not want help. Accepting help meant opening my soul and I was determined not to do that.

Perception

I look back

To the past

There must have been a time

Some long-forgotten time

When happiness prevailed

When a child could laugh

And toss her curls,

Then effortlessly

Launch still another assault

On a world

Not yet grown distant -

Not yet grown dim.

There was such a world,

With depth and

Color and texture.

When eyes

Not yet shackled to their tunnel

Not yet searching for hostile nuances

Fixed their sights on a world

Which shone in splendor

And promised always

Love, and safe deliverance

From the tempests of the night

From the injuries of the day.

But then,

Without warning,

That world was gone.

And disease

Locusts and vultures

Devastated

That small,

Once promising land (1963)

I completed the master's program in comparative literature and decided not to continue for a doctorate. While I loved the program and the challenges it provided, I was still unsure what I wanted for myself. I got a job as an instructor in the English Department at Wayne State and was accepted into the doctoral psychology program for a degree in clinical psychology. This schedule looked like it would keep me busy, doing work I was actually passionate about. I loved the teaching and really enjoyed the students I was working with.

My success in psychological interpretations of literary pieces presented me with the possibility that if I learned more about psychopathology, I could, perhaps, support myself as a writer and, at the same time, find a cure for myself. I told myself that success would be easy. This was what I habitually told myself, and of course, it was generally not easy. Once I began the clinical psychology program at Wayne State, I did what many students do: I diagnosed myself with most of the pathologies I read about. They all fit in some fashion or other. I hoped that the more I knew, the more I might be able to help my own situation. I would not have to open up to another person but I could possibly work out of my mess by myself. Since I had been accepted into a doctoral program in clinical psychology, I thought I was on my way to getting my life in order.

More information did not help; in fact, it only added to my confusion. Outwardly, I continued to function but chaos reigned within. I continued to teach English at Wayne State while enrolled in the doctoral program. I think that part of me was passively hoping that someone would see my struggles and offer to help me. I was working hard, feeling desperate and terribly alone. I was looking for a rescuer…someone who would reach out AND know what I needed AND fill that need. It's as though no part of me wanted to have anything to do with preventing my collision with reality. I still chose not to reach out and no one reached out to me. However, while I wanted someone to reach out, I felt fearful of being found out. The shame would be too much, and so I stayed silent. I was afraid that the people in my sphere of influence would discover that I was an imposter. That I was not the brilliant, well-informed person I presented. I worried that I would be dismissed as a psychological mess. I really believed that remaining in this quagmire was better than giving up any level of control and reaching out for help.

I was now twenty-four years old, still struggling, still working hard, and still unable or unwilling to look at my many successes. If I did pay attention to where I was in life, I would only find failures.I focused on what I deemed to be my failure in Europe. I dwelled on my overwhelming disappointment in not finding the world I sought. Looking realistically at my accomplishments, I would see that I succeeded at almost everything I attempted. This did not seem to register with me. It did not seem to matter to me.

I definitely felt like a failure when it came to therapy. The therapist I was working with had a psychoanalytic focus. I had to do the talking, and I felt mute. I was terrified of the silence in the therapy room. I wanted to break out of the terrifying black hole I felt confined in but was unable to reach out for help. I was afraid that I would strike out in anger. I desperately needed a response from my therapist. It was not forthcoming. We were in different worlds.

I was still living with Mom on a part-time basis and I had become more aware of how needy we both were. I loved Mom. I didn't know how to relate to her. I wanted to leave, but part of me believed I could not survive without her. I felt attached to her so intensely that my very existence depended on maintaining this sick relationship. I knew I needed distance. I needed to move away. I needed to find out who I was, separate from my mother. I needed to learn that I could survive as a separate person. I needed to deal with the war. I decided to move out to Ann Arbor. Implementing this decision was not as easy as it sounds. When would I be ready for this move?

I was completely, utterly depressed. Sleeping was impossible. I stumbled through my days with little personal energy, while keeping up a facade that all was right with my world. I did a good job at work but did very little to take care of myself. I had no interest in eating and felt like I was not even certain that I was alive. I bumped my head into a wall so that I could feel pain and validate that I was a living being who could feel physical pain. I constantly thought about life and death. I didn't think that I could continue my life as it was. I knew that suicide was a mortal sin in my Catholic theology, but I don't think I really cared what the church thought. I was so alone. Finally, I broke down and attempted suicide. As I was playing with the pills I ultimately took, I pondered many things: I didn't want to hurt Mom or my sisters, and I knew this would be hard for them. Why did I want to do this? It was even a sin for a Catholic. Is this real? Would this be a permanent solution? I took the pills.

What a stupid thing to do. I panicked. Why did I do this? Nothing made sense to me. My life was spinning out of control. I feel hopeless. I'm afraid of myself. It would be a waste of my time to continue working at life. This attempt on my life scared me. I became aware that I did not want to die. I called my doctor and asked for help. This was good because it was the first time that I was clear that I wanted to live. I wanted to strike out. I knew I was angry but had no avenue available to express this rage. I was used to being rational. I would take problems and find solutions for them. At this point, I felt angry, but had no idea as to what I was angry about. Talking about feelings did not do what I felt I needed to do. I had taken the pills to numb my anger and wipe out my fear.

This gesture was a call for help, as I had no sooner taken pills than I called my doctor and shared what I had done. I woke up in a hospital and had no idea where I was and what I was doing there. Once I understood what I had done, I agreed to stay for two weeks so I could get some intensive therapy. I thought that I would at least be safe from myself. While there I felt angry at myself but also safe. However, my defenses remained high. The monotony of this time period did give me the opportunity to get a good look at myself. I did not like what I saw. I saw a "kid" who was angry, in pain, whining, and self-destructive, yet unwilling to reach out towards the help that was available. I heard the stories of others who were also in distress and was able to identify with many of these stories. It was helpful to hear about the lives of others in group therapy. I was not alone. After two weeks in the hospital, I was released and continued my work. Nothing had really changed. My workmates thought I had taken a vacation. I was, however, still living on the emotional edge. I continued therapy but felt it was not helping me. Something was missing. I did not inform school and work about my suicide attempt. Again I felt alone with one more secret to keep. I am not sure that I managed to keep my secrets, but I believed I was doing so.

It may seem ironic, but the more intense and destructive I felt, the more skilled I seemed to be when it came to working as a psychologist. As I continued in the psychology program, I got an internship as a psychologist for the Wayne County Juvenile Court when I entered my second year in the graduate program. Yes...even with my limited experience, my classification was Psychologist 1. I began as an intern, and later as a staff psychologist. I did psychological testing and saw some children in therapy. I really enjoyed administering batteries of tests. They were like complex puzzles that provided a wealth of information about the person taking the tests. I enjoyed making the process fun for the children. Teens were another kind of challenge. I put my energy into dealing with their resistance, often with positive results. Most of these kids had had people give up on them over and over, and I was determined not to do that. I felt strongly empathetic for their life situations.

Most of the cases that came to the Clinic for Child Study came from the lower socio-economic classes. Just looking around gave me an education that school cannot provide. What an eye-opener! If I thought I had a hard time as a child, it did not begin to compare with what some of these children lived through.

I was the therapist for a ten-year-old girl. She was adorable…a small black child with a mass of black curls and huge eyes that took in every aspect of her environment. She was affectionate and bounced around the playroom as though she had reached part of heaven. She loved being there and played with all of the toys. They all seemed new to her, so I concluded that she did not have much in her environment to play with. She seemed to have no stranger anxiety and very quickly attached herself to me. She immediately began talking and telling me stories about herself and others. She vacillated between laughter and tears. She had experienced years of abuse and was in her tenth foster home. She was depressed and confused. We spoke about her many experiences in her foster homes and various schools as we played in the playroom. She became attached to a doll and I encouraged her to say loving things to the doll that she herself might want to hear from someone looking after her.

Child to Rosie the doll: "You are a very good girl. I love you."

Suddenly, she vacillated between a loving parent and a violent parent in her play with the doll when she spilled her drink.

Child: "Rosie, you are a very, very bad girl. Look what you did! You made me spill my drink!"

At this point, the child threw the doll and everything within her reach to the opposite side of the room and screamed. She seemed very familiar with the swings between these two kinds of parenting. She had most likely experienced violence in the many homes she had lived in, so this probably felt like normal behavior. I attempted to explain to her that she just made a mistake when she spilled her drink. This was no big deal for most people. For this child, it had been the end of the world. She trembled as she screamed and cried, and melted into my arms as I held her and told her that she was okay and that she was not bad. When her feelings subsided, we role-played what should have happened in "good" families. We talked about "making mistakes being a chance to learn new things, not an opportunity to get abused. Gradually, she became more consistently kind and loving to the doll and transferred this behavior to herself. Her behavior at school and at her foster home improved and according to the court, her therapy was considered over. I felt that she needed much more help and hoped that she would have the opportunity as she got older. On her last session, I gifted her a doll and told her that she could practice being the good parent she now knew she had inside her. She beamed with joy. I believe I was speaking to myself as much as I was addressing this child.

I worked with small children who had been brutally beaten by parents, siblings, and neighbors. Many of the children were homeless with no family to look out for them. Large families lived in one or two rooms with little in the way of furniture or comforts. I worked with court social workers to evaluate a young family with a baby in danger and we warned the court that the child would probably not survive if placed back in the home. The parents were very immature and had no idea how to deal with a young child. They needed support and help with parenting skills. They loved their child but lacked inner control over their own feelings. The court workers needed time to teach these controls in order to safeguard the baby. We presented our case, but the judge released the child to the home. Three weeks later, the baby was dead, shaken by a parent because he wouldn't stop crying. My heart quickens when I think about this child. I still feel guilt and anger. I did my share of what-ifs but nothing changed the outcome. I hated feeling so helpless when it came to intervening in this case. I had to accept that I could make a difference in some cases but not in others.

The court was in a dangerous part of the city, so if we went out for lunch, we needed a guard protecting us until we got to our cars. The neighborhood showed signs of having been a great family neighborhood. The houses were large, with wonderful front porches, and one could easily imagine families gathering on a hot summer evening, watching the youngest amongst them playing on the grass, while the adults were chatting and having drinks. That image is from an age gone by. Those gathered on the porches at this point in time, spewed epithets and shouted menacingly at one another and at anyone daring to walk past the front of the home. Most were drunk or high on drugs. The homes were in a dreadful state of disrepair with porches and, in fact, houses falling apart. Bricks appeared loose and dangerous, and it looked like it had been a long time since a paintbrush had graced the trim. The grass from my fantasy was not there, long since replaced by weeds and dirt. It was sad to see the condition of the neighborhood. The people living in the area were almost entirely black. Many of them seemed unemployed as they sat on the porches all hours of the day or night. I was told that the area was called Black Bottom, and to me, it really did feel like the bottom for the people living there.

This was the middle to late 1960s in Detroit. Race relations were strained to the max. I had gotten tangentially involved with the NAACP a few years earlier as an undergrad when I interviewed several leaders for the Wayne State radio station. I felt strongly that I needed to take some kind of role in expressing my views and advocating changes in racial attitudes. I had no idea what to do or even what a single person could do. I had made some black friends at the court and was incensed with how they were treated in various circumstances. I was, however, incredibly innocent and uninformed. I was not aware that ignorance could lead to growing racism. I asked my friend Robert, a black man, to dinner at my home. Robert responded:

"You live in Grosse Pointe Farms, don't you? Where on earth are you coming from? You ask me for dinner in a city where black people like myself are not allowed after 6 p.m. Do you want me to end up in jail? How could you not think about this? Are you kidding? I don't want to be hard on you, but you need to think this out before making this kind of an invite."

I was shocked. I had no idea what Robert was talking about. I was a racist. I did not know about this law. I had been living in Grosse Pointe Farms for a number of years, a community where black people couldn't even be in the city after 6 p.m. and I did not know this. How could I have been so stupid? How could I have spent years wearing blinders when perceiving the world I was living in? How could I choose to live in an area where good people were treated in such a discounted, hostile manner and not see it? I still can't believe how naive I was. It is amazing to me that I went to a High School and never saw a black student and I didn't even wonder why there were no black students in my school. I realize now that people in the Grosse Pointes just did not talk about this level of racism. That was the way it was and apparently, no one was to question or speak of this terrible rule. It just was, it just existed and people just chose to ignore a terrible wrong. There were undoubtedly many people like myself who had chosen to not know. We didn't pay attention; after all, this rule did not directly affect us. Many of the worst rules are not talked about but are lived with no questions asked. I was guilty. I never wondered why there were no black people in my high school class and that the only black people I saw on the streets were housekeepers for the well-to-do homeowners. I did not question this or even notice it.

"Robert, I am so sorry. I didn't know. I would never want harm to come to you." We continued to be friends and I continued to learn from him, but the relationship did not grow. I remember when I first started taking the bus to the university and I was shocked to see how differently people lived compared to my lifestyle. I was blind then. To this day, I am still shocked as to my blindness when it came to race. I am aware that blindness such as mine perpetuates racial issues.

I did some research work at Lafayette Clinic and when the civil disturbances of 1967 broke out in Detroit, I co-wrote some research articles with Dr. Paul Lowinger on the National Guard and the riots. Our teams were out during the riots, interviewing guardsmen and black militants all over the areas where the most heated conflicts had occurred. I couldn't believe the amount of shooting, but we got our research done. We found extensive racism amongst the National Guard and its leadership. We had three main conclusions. The first was that Caucasian Americans were, on the whole, unwilling to face the racial problem this nation was attempting to deal with. Second, when or if the problem was addressed, it was almost as likely to be seen as a conspiracy of blacks against law and order rather than socio-economic deprivation. The third conclusion was that white Americans often feel powerless as individuals when it came to taking any action to change racial attitudes.

The Guard itself epitomized the racist, segregated aspects of society. In 1968, the Guard was segregated and claimed to have no room to accept blacks. The waiting lists consisted of whites wanting to avoid the draft. We concluded that in 1968, the Guard was a "conservative if not retrogressive force in the struggle of blacks for participation and equality." The Guard was not happy with our work and we made the front pages of the *Detroit News* on New Year's

Day with accusations of racism. I had several generals in my living room that day presenting their case, but we did not alter our findings. Several of our research articles appeared in psychiatric journals and the article on the Guard appeared in *White Racism,* a collection of articles on racism. I was happy to have been involved in this research and to perhaps make an inroad in battling racism.

This was an exciting time for me. I felt I was in a position to make a difference in my world. I felt the energy of the time: the antagonism for the war in Vietnam, the racial battles at home, the political struggles, and at the university, I experienced being immersed in them. I could step out of myself for a time and feel the intensity of the world around me. I felt alive. I was buoyed up by the intensity of the world around me.I didn't have to think about my inner world.

BREAKDOWN AND LIFELINE

I felt reprieved by the intensity of the conflicts around me, since everyone's issues seemed so much worse than mine. In spite of this, I was unable to find a way out of the hell I was creating in my life. It probably wasn't a hell, but I was feeling increasingly suicidal. I was afraid of myself and of what I might do to myself.

Suicide was again in my sights. I played with the pills in front of me as I deliberated my future. "I'm so alone. I'll never feel happy or complete. I don't know what I want, but I'll screw it up anyway. Oh my God…I am being such a victim; I can't stand this whining…I don't want to live like this. But dying is forever. There's no turning back. How sure am I of what I want? Am I just trying to get attention? I counted them…one…two…three. Think of the people who love you and how they will feel if you harm yourself. You may not believe that there are people who love you, but there are!...four…five…six…. Suicide is such an angry behavior. It's really permanent. No coming back. No changing minds. Do you really want to hurt people that much? Will they really care? What am I doing." …seven…eight…nine…ten. Angrily, I took the pills and panicked and moments later called for help. I suddenly knew I did not want to die. I wanted another chance at life.

I woke up again in the hospital. I felt so unhappy, discouraged, and defeated. I had vowed I would never let myself get back into this emotional space. As the days passed, I felt my spirits begin to lift. After one month in the hospital, I returned to my life. Even after trying to work on my issues for a month, I knew that this was not the therapy that I needed. I couldn't make it work for me.

It was summertime and people around me were enjoying their vacations. I was surprised that no one seemed to miss me. I was actually disappointed that no one missed me. I was again surprised that it was important for me that people around me cared about me and missed me. Was I doing this crap to myself to get others to notice me? That was a very distressing thought. I needed to make a major change. I had to find other ways to approach my issues. I stopped therapy with the doctor I had worked with for several years. I did not believe that the therapeutic experience had been helpful.

I had to find a way to dig into my past…to overcome the traumas I'd been trying to run away from. I'd pretended for years that I really didn't have any feelings from way back then…from the war…after all…things had been wonderful then. I had trapped myself. Both the past and the future seemed impossible to deal with. I was stuck.

I needed to find help. I needed someone to help me unlock my past so that I could be free.

A NEW THERAPY MODEL

I knew, however, that I needed help. I had recently heard about a new brand of psychotherapy and wanted to see for myself what it was all about. An Ann Arbor psychiatrist, Stan Woollams, was doing a presentation on Transactional Analysis. I signed up for the presentation and was excited to see this therapy modeled. It was clear to me that this modality encouraged the strong expression of feelings, and I was aware that I really needed help in getting in touch with feelings I had repressed from all of those terrifying years of war and the many traumas that followed. I'm finally willing to look at the war years as an issue I need to deal with. I need to take the "rosy glasses" off and deal with very real pain I experienced in those early years. I was very frightened of the maelstrom of feelings boiling up inside of me. I did not feel safe expressing them. I knew it was time to face these demons; I needed to find a safe place to do so.

The presenter had people talk to parts of themselves, moving from chair to chair. I could almost see what these parts looked like as the patient took turns being each discordant part. Suddenly, I realized that it would feel much safer for me if I could separate out different parts of myself and deal with them one at a time. Perhaps I could even begin to understand some of the conflicts that I felt were driving me. At some point, I could put them together. I also knew that my body was crying out for some opportunity to express the volcano of feelings I was holding in my body. I knew this would make a difference for me, and I was so desperate at this time that I was willing to try anything. I made an appointment with this doctor and began a long and painful 14-year odyssey. At first, I was in both individual and group therapy and very slowly began to tell my story.

My first therapy session with Stan felt terrifying. I began to talk. I had made a commitment to myself to work at this therapy and to be truthful, and over time, I told myself that I would learn to express what was going on inside. Stan's office was very private and it wasn't like I was in an office building and the whole place could hear what I was saying or yelling. In that first session, we talked, and I felt understood. It took me a while, but it was ultimately a place where I first learned to scream and demolish pillows with a bat and a tennis racket. The first time I shouted and used a weapon (a bat) in therapy felt like releasing a bomb. It was an explosion from deep within my core. I don't know why Stan wasn't terrified of me. I know that I was terrified of myself. I went on for what felt like forever, ultimately splintering the bat and turning the pillows into shreds. I was frightened of myself. I had never felt that level of loss of control. When I was finished, I felt completely exhausted. Tears followed my rage, and I cried until I felt emptied. Stan accepted me as I was at that moment and comforted me. His comfort and acceptance seemed more important to me than the work I had done. I had believed that no one could accept the person I was harboring inside of me. I learned that my feelings were good and that expressing them was what I needed to do, and that I could find safe places to let go. I even learned to use my fists while screaming at the people I imagined on the pillows. I had no idea that I held so much pain, fear, anger and rage inside of myself. I wept so much that I feared I would never stop. Over time, I expressed the feelings I had repressed towards the many people in my head. Some of these people were my father, mother, sisters, German soldiers, the father of the children who drowned, Jake, and the list went on and on.

The relief I felt was palpable...I knew I could ultimately free myself from the past which I had allowed to dominate my life. I had been running from the true nature of my past. I had painted such a rosy picture of my life in Europe during the war that I actually returned to Europe in the hope of finding the world of my childhood. I didn't give myself an opportunity to face the reality of what I had experienced. I now understood why I had been so determined to go back "home" to find the world I missed. I also understood why I felt such a deep depression when the world I was looking for was not there. It wasn't real. I became aware that I needed to face the truth of my past, especially the ugly parts, in order to be free. I began to understand the phrase "truth will set you free." My journey to freedom was underway. I knew that to save myself, I needed to have therapy be my focal point and everything else would fall into place.

I was twenty-six years old when I began my journey to health, and I felt like I was beginning a new life. I was in intensive individual and group therapy with Stan. After being in therapy for about two months, I also joined what was a weekend training group to learn how to do Transactional Analysis. I signed a training contract to become a Clinical Transactional Analyst. This meant that one weekend per month (from Friday evening through Sunday afternoon), I would attend a group where those attending would take turns being client and therapist under Stan's supervision. There were about 16 people in the group, all of which were licensed therapists (psychiatrists, psychologists, and social workers). The work would be videotaped and evaluated within the group structure. The person role-playing the therapist could choose to use various therapeutic modalities. Some worked in Gestalt, primal, regressive, analytic, behavioral and more formal Transactional Analysis. Here was an opportunity to work with my feelings in all types of modalities, and then make some sense of things in my brain.

With the amount of time available in the training weekends and therapy weekends, I would finally have the time and setting to do the therapy work I needed to do. When it came to training, in one year, I was eligible to take my board exams. I did so, and I passed. Wow! I was now a Clinical Transactional Analyst. My next goal was to also become a Teaching Member in Transactional Analysis. To be eligible for this level, I needed to have three of my trainees complete Clinical membership and also have board exams. I completed this level in two years and continued teaching and working as a clinician for twenty-eight years. I continued in therapy with Stan Woollams for about fourteen years, and working with him gave me a new life. He helped me save my life. I will forever be grateful for this "unusual" therapy and for this therapist. I find it sad that these therapeutic approaches that worked so well for me never became mainstream. They were never fully accepted by universities and professional associations. They took too much time and energy and money and were not profitable for the insurance companies. These modalities also required special settings. The offices needed to be private, spacious, and soundproofed so as not to alarm neighbors. They needed to have the room for people to spend the weekend in camping-like conditions. The intense therapy work was made safer because participants agreed to stay for the weekend. It was important to stay because leaving in an emotionally upset condition could prove dangerous.

Transactional Analysis made sense to me. I learned that I had three ego states. Each consisted of systems of feelings and their related behaviors. I had often wondered why I sounded and felt like a different person when confronted with various stressful events. I was reacting from different parts of myself. Eric Berne, the founder of Transactional Analysis, called them Parent (P), Adult (A), and Child (C). I tended to react from my Adaptive Child when faced with my father's rage from my Adult when at school or work. I was frequently operating from my Critical Parent when I was berating myself and others. I seldom approached myself from my Nurturing Parent and, in fact, resisted giving myself positive strokes.

When my father flew into rages, it was often his out-of-control Child ego state or possibly his Critical Parent raging at us. He seldom locked into his Adult ego state which could have helped him solve his problems by appraising reality with available facts. With sixteen brothers and sisters, there was little nurturing for him as the second oldest, and as a result, he had very little energy available in his Nurturing Parent ego state for others. He spent most of his time in his angry Parent or angry adaptive Child. Mom spent a good deal of her time in her Nurturing Parent and depressed Child. She tended to placate or please others around her and was out of touch with her own needy Child.

Our interactions revolved around the drama triangle with participants taking the roles of Persecutor, Rescuer, and Victim. We all took turns playing the various roles. An example of this was one time when I forgot to put some groceries away.

Dad (very angry tone): "Didn't your mother ask you to put these away?" (Critical Parent) His eyes were already bulging, his jaw was rigid as he spit out words, and his head was beet red.

Mom (softly): "It's not a big deal…you don't need to sound so angry." (Nurturing Parent) Mom was on the verge of tears, holding her body rigid as she feared an outburst.

Me (crying): "I'm sorry…I didn't hear Mom…I was doing homework." (Adaptive Child)

Dad (angrily picking up the dinner casserole dish and smashing it to the floor): "Maybe now you'll know groceries are important!" (Critical Parent)

Me (thinking): "I can't do anything right. What is wrong with me?" I was blaming myself, but I felt enraged with Dad. I reminded myself I hadn't done my chore and because of my failure, Dad exploded. I felt responsible for his feelings. In our home, Dad was usually the Persecutor and Mom was generally the Rescuer. However, we all learned how to play all of the roles of the games.

I learned about psychological games. I learned to diagram these games I was playing and even to examine the rewards I gained…my payoff. The overall payoff for me was to gain enough bad feelings to justify killing myself. Once I understood the payoff, I was able to uncover the childhood decision I was reinforcing by the game I was involved in.

The outcome of my game-playing or payoff entrenched me even more deeply in the life script I had written for myself. I learned that a life script is a plan (unwritten) that I was creating for myself from the moment I was born. I added decision after decision to this plan as traumatic events unfolded in my life. Good experiences often resulted in positive decisions, and traumas such as the bombings and losing important people in my life brought negative or destructive decisions. The most lethal decisions, such as "I don't want to live" or "feelings are dangerous and I don't want to feel," are the foundations of powerful directives that can drive a script. It was important for me to pay attention to my behavior, learn when I was playing games such as "poor me," "kick me," or "now I've got you, you son of a bitch," and stop myself from collecting the payoff of bad feelings. Moreover, I needed to recognize the feelings I was collecting…what were they? Was I sad, angry, confused? More importantly, I needed to do all of this without kicking myself. When I was sad, I would be angry with myself for feeling depressed. This cycle seemed to be endless.

None of this work was easy, as I had to be aware at all times of what I said or did to myself or others and how I perpetuated my old script or reinforced the new script I was writing for myself. My new script gave me permission to be alive, to be happy, to be successful, and to get my needs met. Staying focused on my behavior, my words, my feelings, and my thoughts was very hard work. It was important for me to realize that I had choices. I could make experiences good for me or bad for me. Examining my life experience in this fashion was not easy. I worked at it; often, I succeeded and at times, I failed, but I persisted.

The hard work for me was looking at my script and deciding that I had the power to change where I was going in life. I would need to make many redecisions in order to change the direction of my life. Some of the directives I had made the basis for my life decisions were: "Don't live, Don't feel, Don't be close, Don't trust, Don't think, Don't succeed, and Don't deserve good things." Some of these messages were given in very subtle ways, while others were given through direct action and words. Some were given by virtue of living through a war. My work was exploring my life and laying bare what these script directives were. I needed to know what I was dealing with. This meant plunging into many very frightening early experiences: seeing them, hearing them, experiencing them to the fullest. At this point, I could put words to the script decision and finally, I was in the position to change it.

In typical fashion, I decided to put my energy into learning more about this type of therapy. It has always been important for me to remain in control. I had generally been resistant to sharing truthfully my life experience, and I needed to be truthful to myself and to the person helping me. Once I experienced the early benefits of Transactional Analysis and redecision therapy, I was thoroughly hooked. I learned how to trust and how to share my deepest thoughts and fears. Trusting set me free to relate to others and to feel happiness.

This sounds like an overload of intellectualism, but this was only a small part of the therapy work. The hardest part was dealing with the rage and sadness in my body. I learned to express pain loudly and physically. I relived old scenes which brought terror and rage alive and screamed and beat pillows. I was given the time and the safe space to relive the past. It was painful, but I am grateful to have found this haven.

Slowly, in fact, after several years, I am feeling better. I am able to see the beautiful world around me. I have friends I can relate to and have fun with, not people I share miseries with. I feel I have moved out of a debilitating depression and can really see and think more clearly. I am happy. I see color and texture in the world. I see the buds on the trees unfurl and become leaves. I hear the birds sing. 1972

MOVING ON

After several years of working for the court and training in Transactional Analysis in Ann Arbor, I decided to move permanently to Ann Arbor and get on with working in a private practice under the supervision of a psychiatrist. I completed my Clinical Membership in TA within one year. I stopped working toward my PhD in psychology. I do regret that I did this, but I decided I only had so much time and I wanted to pursue a program that was personally helpful to me. I enjoyed working with groups and families and felt I could be helpful to others and to myself. I was learning to implement a system that I KNEW would be helpful to the clients I was working with.

I am grateful for the time at the court as it opened my eyes to social issues that persist to this day. I chose to open my eyes to the world around me and see the inequities, the racism, the pain others experienced. I also chose to do what I could to make changes in the world. I decided that no matter how crazy my personal life experiences had been, I could deal with them and I could use my experiences to help others. Many people also had monumental hoops that they had to jump through to get anywhere positive in life and had met with success.

I had found a system I could feel passionate about. I loved the work I was doing and I was very successful at it. I spent summers at the Institute for Group and Family Therapy in California, where I worked with Robert and Mary Goulding and many other therapists from around the globe. Learned about life scripts, redecision therapy, and game analysis. The Gouldings were loving and brilliant. They eagerly shared the wealth of their information. Their specialty was Redecision Therapy and I was able to change many of the very early decisions I had made. I met many wonderful therapists at the Institute and I treasure the time I spent there. I worked with Jacqui Schiff and learned about Reparenting. I learned how to help clients who felt a need to regress to earlier times in their lives and undo some of the tragic early decisions they had made at times of stress. Other experts taught me Primal and Gestalt Therapy. I had always been fascinated by family therapy and was fortunate to get to know Virginia Satir and Ruth McClendon who shared their wisdom as I watched them work with many families and as they supervised my work as a therapist. I was able to experience firsthand all of these modalities and I became quite adept at all these strategies. I loved the positive focus of Transactional Analysis. I also learned how to explore a client's motivations for playing harmful games. While working at these Institutes, I also learned to fully appreciate the physical beauty of the world around me. I worked in the mountains, on the shores of the ocean, in the redwood forests, and in other exquisite, calming locations.

I loved the group therapy sessions as I was able to observe others experiencing pain similar to what I felt and this gave me a tremendous amount of permission to open my heart to my feelings and to express them loudly. Making noise was definitely therapeutic for me, as I had spent most of my years in silence. Groups and marathons were extended sessions from a minimum of four hours weekly to weekends, or to month-long sessions. The extended time made it more difficult to maintain my defenses and provided safety, so it was easier to open up and share. As a group member, I was not alone. I was able to experience my pain surrounded by supportive and loving people who truly understood my suffering. With the help of the modeling provided and the generous permissions, I learned to express my feelings, sometimes very loudly. I destroyed many tennis rackets and pillows, unleashing my rage and it felt good. I took in new parenting messages and they helped me solidify the new decisions I was making. My inner feelings and my voice felt much more in sync. I even learned how to ask for and accept help. I was able to stop taking all medications. This therapy was definitely helping me. I was no longer mired in negative feelings and thoughts. I was beginning to give up my primordial need to be in control of everything in my life, and let others help me.

Some of the therapy I was experiencing involved a system of reparenting and making new life decisions. I relived some of the early traumas in my life. There were many painful times. While re-experiencing those moments, I discovered the pathological decisions I had made under these stressful conditions and made new, healthier decisions. Where I had decided that touch was painful, I was able to give myself permission to enjoy touch. I had spent much of my life suicidal with no commitment to life. After extensively working on these early deadly decisions, I was able to commit myself to life and make a decision that I would henceforth never hurt or kill myself or even attempt these behaviors. All of this took years of pain and joy. It was hard work. I had to decide that I was worth the money I was spending on myself. I spent a fortune and I am worth it. It took me years of painfully sifting through my past. It was not easy. I say this because it sounds like an easy process, as I describe it. It is not easy.

I had to stop memorializing war times as the best times of my life that I wanted to go back to. It was a terrible time, a frightening time, and a time of life or death. In the safety of therapy, I re-experienced the trauma and terror of the nights and days in the air raid shelters with bombs falling around us…the fear of death we all felt. As a child, I had no idea what was happening around me. I only felt the panic in the shelter and saw the terrified looks on the faces of those around me. I relived the sounds….the whistle of the bombs, the quiet whimpering of those around me, the silence of the adults. I remembered my private consultations with God and my pleading for our lives. I felt my mother's body stiffen with each bomb blast and saw the fear in her eyes as she tried to comfort us. As I experienced all of this trauma, I had no idea why these bombs were falling on us, why people wanted to kill us, and why we had to have people we were afraid of and didn't even like, live with us. I think it was important to relive these experiences as a true part of my past, in a safe environment, in order to put them in the past. I had to acknowledge that they were real and traumatic and that I had lived through them, before I finished with them. I was able to take the intense pain out of these memories. I will always have these memories, but I can access them without including the agonizing feelings. I can remember the deaths at the Canadian camp, the loss of our baby, the loss of my father. I can have these memories and know that they are from the past and that my mourning for them is over. I know that I can go on with life and that I have learned from all these tragic moments and that my learnings will help me deal with future tragedies.

I had the time to do all of this painful work. In these groups, there was no "time is up." I could continue until I was emptied of the experience. This type of work took time and patience and I was given both. It took a dedicated therapist who was willing to do this hard work with me. I was often held and stroked until my shaking ended and I could once more speak. Time to work out our pain appears to be a luxury many therapists do not extend to their clients. The ninety-minute group seems useless to me as most people can easily maintain their resistance for this time period. In this type of group, there is really only time to "check-in" with patients. Feeling safe enough to deal with pain takes time. It also takes a special office situation where making noise is not a problem and where schedules are flexible. The weekly groups in my practice were four hours and the weekend groups began on Friday and ended on Sunday afternoon. There has to be enough time for the Child to feel safe.

Reliving these intensely painful experiences, this time feeling safe enough to express the appropriate emotions, and having the Child in me who had lived these times get comfort, made all the difference in my life. Knowing I was not responsible for the awful events in my life made it easier to make new decisions. I did not "bring the war." I was not responsible for my father's drinking and rage. I was not the cause of my Mom's sadness and fear. I did not need to carry this mantle of shame and guilt as I discovered that MY behavior had not been shameful. I had done nothing to be ashamed of.

I also had to stop blaming others for my misery. As long as I saw others as the problem, I could not take charge of my experience. I may not have initiated my issues, however I kept them going and unresolved by blaming the outside world. I needed to look inside myself and forgive. I needed to let go of the people I had remembered as causing the blackness in my world. I had to free myself.

Under stress, it is commonplace to make life decisions that really make no sense and prove to be harmful when it comes to moving on with life. These decisions often include the words "never" and "always," such as "I will never do that again…I will always be a failure…You always make me mad!" "You never tell the truth." I made many of these decisions and in time, I was able to unmake them. I have learned to watch the words I use. I was excited with what Transactional Analysis meant to me personally. I knew very early on in my treatment that this form of self-examination made sense for me, and I knew I wanted to teach others this system. Within three years, I was ready to teach as a fully accredited Teaching Member of the International Transactional Analysis Association.

It was 1972, and one of the new decisions I made was to change my name. My name was Wilfrida Ferdinanda Louisa Huige. I never liked this name and I felt that it contributed to my sense of alienation. I had been named after my grandfathers and felt that the name added to the sense that everyone wanted a boy when I was born. With the new life I was making for myself, I believed I needed a name I chose for myself. A name that would assist me in feeling I truly belonged. I chose Kristyn Anne Huige and I have been very happy with this decision. This name is me. It felt a bit like starting over with a clean slate. I know that this is not actually the case, but it sure felt that way and I felt a surge of energy toward health. I feel cleansed and new…fresh to this world. I was now 29 years old.

A NEW WORLD OPENS UP - 1966-1979

It took some time, but I began to enjoy life. The more I understood about myself and my motivations, the more alive I felt. I was looking around me and discovering that I did have friends and that I could enjoy time spent with these people. I was not alone. In fact, as I looked back at my life, I had never been really alone. I had genuinely felt I had no one who cared about me, but this belief came from the misinformation I had been feeding myself. I was working on evaluating the truth in my life. I had never questioned the negative beliefs about myself. Now, I am confronting them and refusing to let them destroy me. I deserved a kind parent in my head and I was ready to be good to myself.

I had worked hard for years, sometimes with three jobs, and had managed to save a considerable amount of money, even after paying for college and therapy. It was time for me to permanently move out and get a place of my own. I moved to Ann Arbor and when I was about twenty-seven, I bought a new condo. Wow! I loved having my own place. It had three bedrooms and two baths, so I could have people over. It was one of the first homes built in Chapel Hill, so the price was definitely great. The complex had a pool and clubhouse and was located in a wonderful area. I loved this home and felt more grounded. Some of my Canadian family loved coming to Ann Arbor and I even had room for Mom when she visited me. I was still working on separating from her emotionally. I decided I wanted to put down roots in Ann Arbor. Having roots somewhere was vital for me. I needed to find a place where I fit in, where I felt I really belonged.

I was still working in a variety of clinics in Detroit and the surrounding areas. I drove to these places daily from Ann Arbor. I was working way too hard and I wondered why I was pushing myself at this level. I was doing fine when it came to the money I needed. It almost felt like I was driven to work and work. My life was a blur. One day whirled into another and at times, it was hard to remember where I was and where I was going. I was in hyper-drive. There was little time to rest. Sleep did not come easily for me, even if time was available. I was still living all the wars in my life while I slept. I needed to slow down. Where was I going? I knew that what was most important for me was my therapy, and all of these jobs helped me afford the help I needed. Perhaps I could consolidate some of my work and make life easier for myself. I decided to focus my professional life in the town I chose to live in, Ann Arbor. It was now okay for me to take care of myself and slow down.

When I was in my late twenties, I needed to decide what I was going to do with all of this education. I was always one to plunge off the cliff and try new ventures. If one direction didn't feel quite right, there was always another way to go. This modus operandi was at work when it came to choice of occupation. I had been working as a therapist under supervision in a variety of settings, but as I was certified and my TA skills improved, I also began conducting workshops and presenting lectures in various parts of the world, especially at International conferences. I was incredibly nervous, but once I had both my Clinical and Teaching certifications, I knew I had to share what I had learned. I had to let go of my performance anxiety and let go. My workshops became popular. Participants representing universities, hospitals, and private practices asked me if I would be willing to do a workshop for them in their part of the world. I began to enjoy performing in front of crowds and appreciated the showman inside of me. I was presenting valuable information. I learned how to do this in ways that kept the attention of the audience and also entertained them.

I accepted trainees from various parts of the world and supervised their work when I visited and when they sent videos. I conducted these workshops and therapy marathons and trained other professionals for more than twenty-five years. My work drifted into the area of human resources in the business world. The appeal of Transactional Analysis touched many fields of study. I loved to travel and teach. It seemed that international work and travel was part of my DNA. I also had a therapy and training practice at home in Ann Arbor. I learned to enjoy my success and met many wonderful people who became fast friends. I had enjoyed every job I worked, but this was truly my dream job. What made it particularly wonderful for me was that I knew I was good at what I was doing. I was making a difference in the world, and I let myself be aware of the difference I was making in the lives of people I worked with.

Early on, I decided that I wanted nothing to do with hotel life. Most people doing this type of work insisted on hotel accommodations. The thought of spending my nights alone in a luxury hotel felt very lonely and boring to me. I said I would accept the work offered if I could stay with one of the families hiring me. I wanted to experience the lives and culture of the people I was working with. Because of this request, I was privileged to live with many incredible people and I was grateful for this. It was an honor to live with people native to the area I was to work in. They generously took me on sightseeing ventures on my days off, and I got to experience life as they lived it.

On my first trip to Australia, I couldn't believe that I was on the other side of the globe. It was such a different world. Even the land was a different color from what I was used to. A rose-colored dirt permeated the landscape. Around Sydney, everything was bright green and very lush. The water was a deep, mystical blue and the sun seemed to be a bright daily fixture in the heavens. I loved the people. They were fun-loving, friendly and very open about themselves and eager to learn. The mountains around Sydney were called the "blue mountains" by the aborigines. They were truly blue as one gazed at them from a distance. I was stunned by the magnificence of the vistas. The scenery was varied and breathtaking. I loved the Sydney Opera House and the beauty of the coral reef. My schedule involved working for three or four days and then time off to sightsee.

The next stop was Melbourne. This city seemed more like an industrial town. It didn't have the exotic feel about it that Sydney had, but it had its own brand of beauty. Again, I was blown away by the generosity and kindness of the workshop participants. The city was quite cosmopolitan and more focused on business ventures.

The third stop for me was Adelaide. I really loved South Australia. This area seemed like "country" to me. I visited animal sanctuaries, opal mines, and Kangaroo Island. My new friends and I camped on Kangaroo Island and walked on the beaches amongst huge elephant seals, seals, penguins, and other wildlife. Camping in a VW bus with a family of five was a new experience for me, but we really had fun. I treasured this time. Although all of Australia was easygoing, this was an even more relaxed part of the country. I had left a winter snowstorm at home in Michigan and in Australia, I enjoyed the warmth of summer. Actually, at times, I felt it was too hot for me, and as no one had air conditioning in their homes, I had to brave the heat in the same fashion as the Australians did…in the pool.

In Adelaide, the nearby desert and adjacent scrub lands were like paintings created by the Aborigine painters. I purchased several of these paintings and they perfectly capture the multiple shades of pinks and browns and greens. The scenes were always crowned by magnificent blue skies. The wonderful local people I stayed with took me to many interesting places. At the Cleland reserve, we played with kangaroos, emus, and cockatoos. I even held a koala bear, whose claws played havoc with my arms, but the experience was worth it. There was an incredible collection of wildlife. I loved my time in Australia.

I made friends with some wonderful people. Robin was a social worker who headed the Boy Scouts for all of Southeast Asia. His was a story of overcoming a car accident as a teen that almost took his life and left him with serious burns all over his upper torso. His face looked like it was almost burned off. When you first saw Robin, it would be easy to say a quiet "wow" and back away. Within an hour of relating to him, you no longer saw the scars, but you saw the glorious soul of this beautiful human being. Robin remained a friend until his death several years ago. Val, his wife, still lives in Adelaide and we communicate through Facebook. Tricia, a good friend from Sydney, is one of the brightest and funniest people I have ever known. She was an event planner for the Australian Broadcasting Company, putting on events such as New Year's Eve in Sydney Harbor. I made so many friends and I loved it that I saw them on a yearly basis. The only regret I have is that I am not good at staying connected with people I meet and love. I think about them, but when it comes to corresponding, I am terrible. I'm still working on this issue. It is never too late to change behavior. I haven't done it yet.

Many other trips followed, including a strictly vacation trip to Africa, primarily Kenya and Tanzania, and the opportunity to visit the Oldivi Gorge, the cradle of mankind. It is a huge crater, about a mile deep and five miles in diameter. It is an area rich in wildlife. It was also dangerous and it was clear that leaving our vehicle was not something to do if we wanted to remain alive. On one tour in the gorge, a friend had to go to the bathroom and her only option was to exit the jeep. After pondering her dilemma for a while, she knew she had to do what nature demanded. She did her duty right next to the vehicle as we all turned away to give her some privacy. She got back into the jeep just in time as a lion had spotted her and was quickly approaching. In Kenya, we met various tribal peoples, such as the Masai and Kikuyu. It was interesting to observe social relationships in these groups. We saw herds of elephants and were continuously on the watch for lions and other big cats. I was again surprised by the number of the animals we saw. We saw a lake full of brilliant flamingos as their mating season was getting underway. Amazing.

I visited Europe three times a year. I usually would work in three or four countries on each trip. I once more had a chance to practice my Flemish, Dutch, and French. It was a much different experience for me than my earlier visit in my early twenties. I was no longer looking for the home I had lost when we moved to the United States. When I visited with my family, I was concerned that the trip I had taken when I was 22 had left a bad memory. Nothing could have been further from the truth. They greeted me with hugs and kisses and expressed how proud they felt of me. What a wonderful experience.

I had learned how to harness the power of my Adult ego state. I was able to stay in the present. I stayed away from the child within me who, occasionally, was still yearning for the past. I have to admit that I did not feel this yearning anywhere near the intensity of the past. I focused on the child within who was creative and knew how to play. I enjoyed the present. I got to know many wonderful friends. The organizations that hired me also made my life easier by hiring translators for the times when speaking other languages proved difficult. When I traveled for work, I was able to enjoy the cities…the beauty of the old buildings, the gardens, the city centers, and the churches, and most of all, the people. At first, it was as though a veil had been lifted from my eyes. I felt connected to the world around me.

Working with clients in these varied cultures expanded my awareness that scripts were cultural, familial, and individual. I enjoyed learning about different approaches to childrearing and the impact these different styles had on individual scripts. Living with people native to the country I was visiting gave me a living tableaux of parenting styles. Not only did I broaden my life experience, but I gained so many good friends. I learned how to have fun and play, something I had known very little about. I even learned how to relax around all kinds of people.

SCHOOL AGAIN 1972-73

Since I only had master's degrees in comparative literature and psychology, I couldn't operate independently as a psychotherapist in Michigan, so I decided to get a master's in social work, where I could work without supervision. I wanted to become an independent practitioner. I signed up for the MSW program at the University of Michigan to get a license. I have been asked what I thought about the program and I have to admit that I didn't really give it a chance. I was over-prepared for the program and was bored a good deal of the time. I took the classes I needed but there was not much new for me. Very few of the classes excited me. I did enjoy my internship, a simulation games class, and discussions with some of the professors, especially Frank Maple. Thinking about the program in recent times, I probably should have gone for the PhD in some brand of clinical social work.

My best experience at U of M was the internship I had at University Hospital on 7 East, where staff members were working intensively with infants who failed to thrive. It was a much different experience than reading about this issue in a text. I learned about infant bonding and the effects on the child when the bond is not there. These babies looked like the starving children in third-world countries. Their eyes were huge and vacant. Their bodies didn't mold into mine when I held them. They didn't cry for food and it was unclear to me whether they even felt hunger. What could make a child give up at such a very young age? Working with the mothers and babies was painful but gratifying. I'd never realized the importance of directly looking into the eyes of the baby. It feels instinctual to me to bring the baby's face close to my own when talking or laughing with the child. Many of the mothers involved did not do this. They often fed their child while they were watching TV with the baby facing the TV, not the mom. I felt the emptiness of the relationships in my gut. It was painful and incomprehensible. These children were not physically abused. They were simply not acknowledged as living human beings. What was wonderful in this experience was that many of the moms were teachable. They took in suggestions and modeling and in time, the babies began to respond. Eye contact, touch, and talking to the baby do make a difference in enabling the connection needed to thrive.

The other experience at the university that was incredibly meaningful for me was the class in simulation games. My classmates and I played roles as members of various socio-economic and cultural groups and were presented with typical life problems. In one game, I ended up playing the role of a black woman in the lowest socio-economic level. I was shocked at the intensity of feeling I experienced when my progress was blocked at every turn. I tried to get a job, rent an apartment, go to school, and I was prevented by lack of money, lack of credit, and various kinds of prejudice. I had no medical insurance and an illness often led to a loss of job, which led to loss of credit, which led to loss of living space, etc. No matter what I tried, there was a roadblock to my success. I can't believe how frustrated and angry I began to feel. I had always believed that if I worked hard, I could gain success. It didn't work here. I was ready to lead a rebellion. I was even ready to break the law. I kept telling myself, "This is only a game." It didn't work for me. While playing the game, I felt totally in this role and the feelings I had were explosive and frustrating. I really learned that people need hope that life can change. Everyone needs a road up or a way out. All hell can break loose when that hope is not there. This was also an important lesson for a therapist to learn, as everyone needs hope that their endeavors will bring some of what they want. Also, people also need to feel that they can have some impact on their world. Most important of all, people need to have choices. Continually facing a dead end leads to civil unrest or depression. I'm beginning to feel hope myself. I am also beginning to believe that I have an impact on the world. I know I have choices and I am liberated. It is really uplifting.

While attending school and working in my practice, I continued getting a considerable amount of additional training in group and family therapy outside of school and worked with a number of top experts in this area. I loved going for many summers to the Western Institute for Group and Family Therapy in California to work with my fast friends and mentors, Bob and Mary Goulding. This is where I came to life, where I found myself, where I came to love myself. I worked with others who also became friends, Virginia Satir, Muriel James, and many well-known therapists. I studied Neuro Linguistic Programming and found some of it useful and all of it interesting. Most of these wonderful people became my mentors. I loved having people who accepted who I was and who were willing to help me learn. I became aware that I had strong skills as a therapist. I felt I could zone in on clients and could intimately relate with them at levels they could understand. I could feel people's pain and help them alleviate it. As I was bathed in love from these mentors, I was able to trust and honestly express my feelings. I was also able to accept myself and all the issues I had been so ashamed of. As I was growing personally, I was also growing as a therapist.

I loved the praise I received from many sources. I was, however, ill at ease with all these compliments. I had spent years feeling undeserving of this kind of attention and I was distressed to discover that this discomfort was still with me. In the past, I would find myself dragging my feet and holding back just to make it clear to people who said "good job" that they were wrong. Now, I decided to charge forward and internalize the praise. I was working hard, and doing a good job, and I deserved to internalize the kudos coming my way. I needed to let myself feel that getting rewarded for doing a good job was okay. I am still working on this. I continued to build my private practice and to travel to exciting places. I loved what I was doing.

PUTTING DOWN MORE ROOTS - 1967-1979

After living in my condo for several years, I decided I wanted to find a place where I could do groups out of my home. It was 1970 and I needed a bigger place. I found a Frank Lloyd Wright home on three acres, with 300 feet of frontage on the Huron River. The home was made of Tennessee ledgerock and glass and was several hundred feet above the Huron River in beautiful woods. This was probably my favorite home of all time. The floor plan was open. There were windows galore. I loved the walls of windows which brought the outside in for me. The rooms were large and the home was "open concept" before this trend was popular. The woods provided the privacy I wanted and needed. A large deck spanned the length of the home and gave me the sense of being in a tree house. The walk-out lower level was perfect for group therapy. There was a massive open fireplace which warmed both the living room and the dining room. The group room also had a wonderful stone fireplace.

I bought it, moved in, and promptly began to redesign the kitchen and dining areas. I added a step-down library with a wonderful fireplace to my master bedroom. I found a roommate who had been a good friend for years. She had been my supervisor at the hospital and was also one of my trainees. We ended up with two great dogs. Geri had a black poodle, and I had a golden retriever. We were housemates until she got married. Geri and Fred, her husband, remained fast friends until their deaths several years ago.

I stayed in this home from 1970 to 1977. While this home was perfect for me and for my practice, the neighbors did not like the traffic my practice brought to the neighborhood. My clients always parked in my circular drive, but one group of neighbors did not like the added traffic on the dirt road. I was fearful of offending them and they threatened to sue, so I decided to sell. I was not completely cured of my need to please people and my fear of people who happened to be unhappy with me. My neighbor, who was doing the same kind of work as I, decided to stay and nothing came of the complaints. I regretted this sale, but I moved on. I was still very fearful of other people's anger.

When I was thirty-seven, I sold the Huron River home and bought another home on Valentine Road with thirteen acres. The property consisted of a separate building that provided a 1,200 square foot office, and a 5,000 square foot house. I wanted more privacy to work with my clients and this office was perfect. This home was surrounded by large oak trees and opened out to a small lake. It was a perfect spot to do the weekend training, therapy, and family marathons. The home was made of fieldstone and cedar, with a large deck. On the lakeside, there was a large, sunny, stone patio. Inside, there were two fireplaces and a wood burner stove. When I moved in, I immediately installed a new kitchen made for a chef. I was ready to create a wonderful family home. I also remodeled the master bath, as the old bath looked like it belonged in a bordello with flocked red wallpaper and a shower which did not work. The new bathroom had a beautiful, huge jacuzzi, new cabinets and all-new plumbing.

I had always wanted children of my own but it was in this home, with its abundance of space, that I intensified my thinking about creating a family through adoption. There were so many children with no families or homes, and here I was, rattling around in this huge place. I wanted a family. I wanted children. I was tired of waiting to get married. I grew up with the frame of reference that marriage came first, then children. Until my therapy experience, I had believed that I was unfit to parent kids, especially those with emotional issues. Now, I believed that my experience would make me a good adoptive parent. I had learned a good deal about stress, trauma, and loss, and perhaps I could provide a home and the emotional support that children needed. It was a bit late to look for a husband. I had friends, but no one I was intimate with. I was told that my success at work tended to intimidate potential partners. I have no idea if this was true. It also did not help that deep down inside of me, I was timid and fearful of intimate relationships. I yearned to have a family, but this goal seemed out of sight.

ADOPTION?

It finally dawned on me that life provided NO DRESS REHEARSALS. There are no practice years. There are NO DO-OVERS. Once a day is lived, it is OVER! OVER! OVER! I could no longer say, "Oh, one of these days, I will get myself together." If I wanted a family, I had to decide NOW and get it together NOW. Once more, I needed to take the leap and trust in myself. I was now thirty-nine years old and not getting any younger. Waiting to fall in love and get married seemed too time-consuming. It also did not seem like something I really wanted to do. Putting my energy into searching for a mate did not appeal to me and I was getting older. To be honest, I was terrified of the possibility of a sexual relationship, despite many years of therapy. I didn't want to wait until I was cured of these fears as I was not sure that it would ever happen, and I was tired of waiting. I could, however, put some thought into adoption as even the age limit to become an adoptive parent was approaching. There are many ways to make a family. Since I was not married, my avenues for adoption were severely limited. In the late '70s and early '80s, local adoptions demanded marriage; however, international adoptions were not as restrictive.

This ruminating about family had gone on for years. I had wanted children since I was very young. I felt the issue became more urgent as time moved on and I got older. I had never believed that a child had to be mine biologically for me to feel maternal love. I also didn't believe that I had to be perfect to provide the love of a mother to children. Adoption had always made sense to me and in my travels, I had become aware of the myriads of children waiting for someone to love them and care for them. The universe has given me so much in terms of emotional support and physical comforts. It was clear to me that I wanted to share what I had. If I was going to wait until I was pathology-free, I would never have a family. I knew I was still imperfect and would remain that way. Children, I discovered, are capable of dealing with imperfect adults. If I adopted a child, we would learn and grow together. I also thought that whatever we made of our lives together, it was bound to provide more opportunities for success for children I would adopt than what lay ahead for them in their birth country.

I was warned by my friends in Transactional Analysis not to do this as it would destroy the therapy practice I had built. I knew that they were right in that my lifestyle would have to be different. I thought that the word "destroy" was a bit hyperbolic. I didn't see creating a family as destructive to my life but as building on my life. I was ready to accept the challenges motherhood would bring. Of course I had only a limited idea what these changes to my life would mean. In some ways there was still a considerable amount of naivete in my thinking. I didn't imagine the dramatic changes a family would make in my traveling lifestyle. I had no idea what it would be like to be a single parent. I also had no idea how stressful caretaking a very large property could be. Add to that the providing and caring for children who were dealing with their own traumas. It's probably a good thing that parents are blind to the real changes and challenges that parenting brings or we might have many fewer children on this earth.

In 1978, I began a research project on foreign adoptions. Eight families who had adopted from Eastern Europe and Central America called me on hearing that I was interviewing adoptive parents who were having issues with their children for a research project. I planned on writing an article about the pros and cons of foreign adoption. These families had come to me because they were unable to deal with a child they had adopted who was having a difficult time. Most of the parents were afraid of the child's rage. They were not prepared to deal with a destructive, and they feared, homicidal child. Most of the children were experiencing issues with bonding. They were acting out, stealing, and attacking parents and siblings physically. I was aware of the literature which described some of the most prominent issues. I was surprised, however, to discover the intensity of these problems in these particular families.

Several of the families came to their first session having already decided that the adoption was not working and the child would be returned to the state children's services. They were terrified of their child and feared that they would be killed by the child. The children in these families were between the ages of eight and fifteen, and most had been in their adoptive families for one year or more. The issue that frightened most of the parents was the rage which seemed never-ending. I taped these families as they told their stories and I could see that many of these loving people were in over their heads when it came to parenting these children. I wondered why they had agreed to my interviews. Some admitted that they came for the free therapy, as I did not charge for these sessions. As the sessions progressed, it became clear to me that some were looking for permission to say goodbye to a child they had welcomed into their homes with love.

I was surprised by how negative the adoptive experience had been for these people. I think that part of the issue for them was that they had expected a child who would be grateful for being adopted. They were unprepared for a child who was grateful for a week, but needed at some point to express feelings bottled up for years. They were also not ready for children who were so terrified of closeness.

Some of the children had spent their early years in orphanages and had very little opportunity to attach to a caregiver. To suddenly be thrust into a family where hugs, touching, and constant interaction were commonplace was not what the children felt comfortable with. They were unable to bond with these people who had opened up their homes in the hope of creating families for themselves. The children needed some distance, and the parents were not prepared to give this distance. Different languages and cultures were also issues when it came to understanding one another. Two of the families decided that with the help of our discussions, they now had the tools to work with the child they had adopted. The other families decided to undo the adoption. I chose not to continue this research project. I must admit that I felt discouraged and somewhat fearful. My eyes, however, were really open to the potential problems facing an adoptive parent.

This experience was an eye-opener for me. I wanted to adopt and had assumed that all would go well. I was grateful that I was a therapist, experienced in scripts, family scripts, game analysis, and early childhood issues. I did not expect a smooth transition. I did expect an early honeymoon period when all was wonderful, followed by testing of limits accompanied by moments of rage and sadness. If I did adopt, I knew it would not be easy. Was I ready to take this on?

DECISION TIME

It was now 1979, and the next trip I was taking would see me go around the globe. I could focus my thoughts on family and what I would need to change to make my lifestyle practical to have children. In some ways, I had been living life in the fast lane and a lot of my life was taking place away from my home. I started this trip in Belgium, going back to the beginning for me. I was now able to experience how difficult my early years had been during the war. I was no longer under the delusion that the war years were the best years of my life. It had been a frightening time and I could acknowledge the terror we had lived with. At that time, Mama was actually a single parent and, in spite of the war, she did a great job with us. Being a solo parent seemed less of a problem for me when I thought about my experience with Mom. She managed, I would also. I did remind myself that my experience with my biological Mom, the person I had always lived with, would be quite different from my taking on unknown children from another country. France was the next place I worked, and I remembered my post-graduation trip and my feeling of failure when my past could not provide the comfort I craved. I reminded myself that I was in a different personal space now.

I thought about the children I wanted to adopt and the cultural shock they would experience when moving to the United States. Probably, some of their experiences would mirror what mine had been. I thought that my experience would actually be helpful in the children's transition. I had come to understand the complexities of moving into a different language and culture and I might be able to help children experiencing similar problems. I had also lived through a great deal of early trauma and that might also give me some understanding of what orphaned children might be experiencing. It was a challenge to focus on the work at hand. I drifted between the many different phases of my life. Then, the place that opened my eyes: India.

I was working in India teaching Transactional Analysis to the Human Resources Department of a company that made boxes. Right outside the doors of where I was working and where I was living, I saw poverty that was beyond anything I had ever experienced. My eyes were opened to very real misery and very real joy. There were crowds everywhere. I saw children with missing limbs begging in order to financially support their families. Some families will go to the extreme of maiming a child so they will be a more successful beggar. These are people who saw no way up from their lowly position in life. Most of the people I saw wore tattered clothes and were involved in various kinds of business enterprises which provided minimally for them.

Everybody seemed to be hawking something on the streets. The numbers of people were overwhelming. I saw multitudes of colors, heard loud noises, and was overwhelmed by the smells of foods, animals, people, and decay. Some of the scents were absolutely horrible, but some were incredibly delicious. Cows seemed to wander everywhere as they were sacred and could not be disturbed. No one adhered to any of the social rules with which I was familiar. There appeared to be no individuals controlling the animals. Cars drove and stopped wherever the driver wanted. I was given a driver and a Mercedes for my use while I was there. My driver drove on whichever side of the road he wanted to be on and stopped wherever he wanted to stop. To my eyes, chaos was ruling. I was really grateful I didn't have to drive. There was so much to take in that I felt overwhelmed by all of the events, colors, smells, sounds, and other stimulations surrounding me. How does one adapt to this?

None of the Indian people seemed to be limited by what I experienced as this "dysfunctional" lifestyle. When I took a closer look, I did see that many of the people I was feeling sorry for looked like they were quite happy. They were used to crowds, pushing, chaos, and shouting. Orderly process seemed more of a Western style. I was staying with a wealthy family who lived in a posh apartment above the crowds of people. I once asked a family member how he felt about the poverty and pain of humanity just outside their window. He responded with surprise and had no idea what I was asking about. He did not even see the struggles taking place just outside his windows. Even though he lived an orderly existence with space for himself and servants to provide the niceties, he was accepting of the chaos, poverty, and pain that reigned just outside his home. It became part of the background he no longer experienced. In fact, I don't believe he even saw the pain I saw. It was simply the Indian way of life. He had become accustomed to a life with blinders protecting him from the world. Seeing the totality of the world would have been overwhelming.

This made me think about life in Grosse Pointe Farms, where I was oblivious of the discrimination just outside my door. I lived with it. I chose to remain ignorant of the racism I was surrounded by. I chose to not see what was in front of me. It was not there. In fact I didn't educate myself about its existence and accepted the status quo without a second thought until it hit me squarely between the eyes in my personal life. Perhaps this behavior is true worldwide. We all stay uninformed until reality touches us personally.

As I learned to accept the chaos in India, however, I continued to be concerned about the plight of the children, many of whom were orphaned and had to fend for themselves. I spent the rest of my time watching life around me and making decisions concerning my life. I needed to help and make a difference. I would adopt and probably adopt children from India.

This trip included work in Belgium, France, India, Australia, and New Zealand. It was a trip that was definitely different from others I had taken as my mind was possessed with thoughts of adoption and I was observing the children everywhere I went. I loved traveling internationally and working with different cultural groups. I had always wanted a family with children. The more I worked with families, the more I thought about creating a family of my own. I was, however, single, and single people did not have much luck when it came to adoptions and I was still ambivalent.

Although I was very successful professionally, I was still working hard sorting out my psyche. Here I was, traveling the globe while dwelling on possible massive changes in my own life. Were my mentors right that adopting children would put an end to my international career? Was I ready to abandon my international career if motherhood demanded it? Did I want to risk setting myself up for failure? Did I trust myself to do what made sense for me? Was I ready to deal with children who had dealt with the pain of loss or worse, the suffering of war? I had many questions I needed to find answers to, and I was determined to find them.

My time in India got me thinking about family again, that I was not getting any younger, and that I would probably adopt from India. My time in New Zealand gave me a chance to touch my mystical side. I was asked to work with a group of Maori who had lost the therapist working with them in a plane crash in Antarctica. They deeply mourned her and their rituals seemed to bring her back emotionally. The intensity of their feelings and their love really touched my soul. There was something about the wailing and praying that suddenly I knew what I wanted and needed to do for myself. I felt from the depths of my soul that creating a family was the right thing to do. I had heard and felt my heart wailing for the kind of love the Maori family group experienced. These people were not alone. Their love connected them. They were connected by their tribal lines, their friendship lines, and their family lines.

I wanted these connections for me as well. I knew I was ready. I knew that part of my reason for wanting a family was because I did not want to be alone. I knew I could provide a better life for children than what they would experience if they remained in an orphanage. I decided it was also okay for me to get something out of this committed family experience. No matter what happened, I would find a way to make things work. I was excited thinking about the coming changes in my life.

I'm ready! Ready for family and new adventures.

I did a good deal of researching adoption agencies.. While I was researching, a friend of mine was also looking into foreign adoption, and she had success with an agency working with El Salvador. I looked into this group and decided to go with Project Orphans Abroad, and with Salvadoran children.

I applied, and the red tape started. Letters and more letters, inspections and more inspections, interviews and more interviews. It seemed that they wanted to know every single detail of my life…and they did…with good reason. I contacted the State of Michigan and a social worker did a home study and concluded that my home would be a great place for two children. I had applied to adopt in the fall of 1980. I was matched with two children. I had asked for two girls, 3 to 5 years of age. In March of 1981, I received a letter that I was accepted as an adoptive parent and the letter was accompanied by a photo of my prospective children. The photo was of two children, one small girl of five with a confused look on her face and a young boy of eleven with a stern, confused, "I'm in charge" look on his face. I loved them both at first sight. They were not two little girls, but I loved them already. These were my children. I felt a tear trickle down my face as I felt myself welcome them. My new journey was beginning. I was excited thinking about what the future would bring me and my new family. I'm ready for a new phase in my life.

The war in El Salvador became more violent, and it was recommended that I not fly to the orphanage to pick the children up. It was too dangerous. The director of the agency I was working with said she was going down with an assistant to pick up a number of children who were waiting for new homes. She would bring my children to me. I had really wanted to pick them up in their home country and get to know them in places that were known and familiar to the children, however, that was not possible now. On May 9, 1981, Mother's Day, I became a mother. I picked my children up in Cleveland, Ohio, at the home of the agency director. My new adventure was beginning. Life was definitely getting more and more exciting and fulfilling.

POSTSCRIPT

The question comes up at this point: "What happened to the other girls? The sisters?" There were three of us and we remained best friends. We have been through thick and thin together. We have shared traumatic events and joyous ones. We were together when we were uprooted. We experienced events that are beyond the comprehension of children, both in war and during peace. We did not understand. We were bewildered. We were frightened. We looked for support and found it in one another. We had our share of battles but resolved them. Our love for each other remained strong.

But what happened to Ria and Corrie? Ria remained in Canada for a while after the rest of us moved. She went to boarding school in Canada and finished high school. She moved home and fell in love with an older man who broke her heart. To take her mind off of her sadness, she joined my Mom and Dad as they went to the wedding of the daughter of one of Dad's friends from Europe. While there, she met a young Dutchman and their relationship flourished. After a short while, they married and Ria moved to the Niagara area in Canada and became a Canadian citizen. Within a few years, they had three children, two boys and one girl. This marriage failed when the children were teenagers because Ria's husband had an affair with Ria's best friend, and because Ria had a problem with alcohol, prescription drugs, and smoking. Ria experienced a good deal of emotional pain but she did not seek psychiatric help. Mom moved in with Ria when her children were teens, and she helped raise the three teenagers. Ria relied on pills which her doctor supplied for her for back pain. As time went on, she was madly in love with the six grandchildren who came along. We stayed connected by telephone and by visits. She always remained aloof and set herself apart during gatherings. As we were growing up, we had often asked, "Where is Ria?" That question persisted. At family gatherings, she would sit away from others because she smoked, and most people didn't want to be near the smoke. As a child, she used books to keep herself separate; as an adult, it was cigarettes. Ria was severely traumatized when Mom died. It was as though she lost the will to go on with life. She and Mom had been so close she couldn't bear losing her. I loved her but I didn't really know what was in her heart. She died a few days shy of her eightieth birthday.

Corrie left home after Dad died. She went to nursing school and lived at the school. Once she graduated, she and a friend took jobs in locations around the United States. Once she managed to leave home, she stayed away. After a few years, she joined the Air Force and soon became a captain. She served for four years, a good deal of it in the Far East: Korea, Taiwan, and Vietnam. She loved the Air Force and it gave her the close family she had always wanted. She really bonded with her colleagues and some of them are still friends now, in their late seventies and eighties. She took risks and was plagued by depression and back pain. Corrie did get therapy and it was helpful for her when it came to dealing with the past. She married a man with a son. Her husband was narcissistic: he was only interested in his own wants and needs. The marriage was unhappy and lasted seven years. Several years later she met Chris, and they married. She had to be repeatedly told that she deserved the good things Chris gave her. Before she fully decided it was not scary for people to be good to her, she would call me, distraught over someone being kind to her. She has been happy in this relationship and now has the happy family she has always craved. Chris's grown daughter moved to Atlanta, so Corrie and Chris followed as there were now two grandchildren to help with. They have had ups and downs in their health, but they are wonderful with each other. In Atlanta, they have been involved with the prison system, bringing the word of God and other gifts to prisoners. Covid curtailed this ministry and it has not resumed. They had been choir members but that was also curtailed by Covid. They are ready to resume this ministry. They are both avid travelers on Viking river and ocean excursions. Life is good for them. Corrie did her share of struggling with the past and therapy was helpful for her. She also became a psychotherapist after she left the Air Force. At this point, she is retired and enjoying her gardens. She never had children of her own, but now enjoys her step-daughter and two grandchildren.

What happened to John? He married Henrietta and they had three children. John became an engineer, and worked on some fascinating projects. One of these projects was a telescope which was situated on a mountain in Hawaii. Corrie tended to have the most contact with John and his family, as he was her godfather. PTSD did not give John a pass. He had issues with alcohol, ulcers and anger. When he reached his eighties, he had mellowed, stopped drinking alcohol and seemed in a good place emotionally. They had four grandchildren. When Henrietta developed dementia, you couldn't find a better caretaker than John. He looked after her every need and never complained. After Henrietta's death, life was more difficult for John. He developed serious kidney disease and was on dialysis. He died at age 90.

What about Mom (Mama). I think that in my mind I never forgot Mama. She has remained one of the strongest people I have ever met. She was my hero during the war. I could always count on her and she never disappointed me. Her world and my world changed once we were in the United States. She also had to learn a new language. She no longer had a position of power in the family as my father took over. She had to learn how to look after people in the bar and she also did the bookkeeping. She still looked after us. She was living with an explosive person and did what she could to keep him under control. She was now dependent, and she was not used to this status. She had been her own person from the time that she was young. In America, she had to ask for rides to any place she needed to go, all decisions had to be approved, she did a job that she did not like, and she had to raise 3 children who were troubled by horrible past experiences. While doing all this, she also had to deal with the death of her parents, and all of the trauma of war that she did not deal with.

Because of her husband's health, she agreed to move to another country, Canada, and found herself more isolated than ever. The hard work never ended. She and her children were overworked and she saw no future in this new situation. She was 30 miles away from anything she could call a town and she could not drive. There were tragedies, especially the loss of a baby boy she had looked forward to greeting. Dad's alcoholism and diabetes drove them to sell this place and it was back to the United States. Dad did not live long after moving back to another bar and a house. As a widow, Mom looked after herself, and within a few years, she decided to move to Canada and help Ria raise her children. Ria had divorced and was having issues with her children. Mom lived with Ria until she died at 82 years of age. She was very happy in her retirement, living with a daughter, grandchildren and great-grandchildren. She was happiest when she was around children.

PTSD AND WORLD WAR II

Children in World War II were looked after by terrified, loving parents who did their best under unbelievably difficult circumstances. Surrounded by bombings, destruction and even death, parents had to hold on to their own sanity and still be present for their children. My mother, a child in World War I, was not helped with her past traumas of this war, but still did her best when it came to caring for 4 children and numerous adults during World War II. She suffered from what psychotherapists would now call Post Traumatic Shock Disorder. In spite of anxiety and depression, she provided amazing guidance during the war, but had trouble finding herself when she lost all of the familiar people in her life. She had to participate in a move she did not want, to be with a man she did not really know. My siblings and I did not experience the tremendous pain and loss that children in Hitler's death camps experienced, but we still suffered from PTSD after the war. We discounted our pain, as did everyone else in our lives. We needed help but were told to forget about the past and just not talk about it. "The memories and nightmares will go away." We stayed silent. We suffered. The memories and nightmares did not go away.

All four of us, American citizens, experienced terror during the war. My brother, John, who was a teen, dealt with his fear by joining the underground and later the United States Army. He needed to have an impact on the world around him. Taking charge, even in a limited way, allowed him to feel less helpless. My two sisters and I were small children, and we relied on the adults around us to provide protection. We had no explanations for what was happening around us, not that saying anything would have made sense of what was happening. The adults around us could not fix what was happening to all of us on a daily basis. They attempted to assure us that there would be an end to our scary days, but it was hard to believe what they said. It seemed to me that what we were doing was hiding and hoping that we guessed correctly when and where we chose a place to hide.

When the war ended, we had a year or so to move on with our lives and hopefully forget the past. I wet the bed and had terrible nightmares. Ria was withdrawn, quiet and pretty much kept to herself. Corrie was confused. We were all agitated, but we were beginning to come out of our distress when my father, who had been absent the entire war, returned to Belgium. I came to understand that he demanded that we go to the United States with him or he wanted a divorce. We had finally begun to feel somewhat at ease, and we were being uprooted and stressed once more. None of us knew this person who was uprooting our somewhat settled way of life.

We left Belgium and all of our wonderful extended family, our beautiful house, our school and our familiar language. I think about all of the Ukrainian children who must leave all that is familiar to them in 2022. Going to a new world means unfamiliar sites, smells, sounds, and people. It means adapting to a totally different culture. Children with PTSD have experienced disaster, loss, and violence. They are trying to forget the graphic scenes they left behind. They want order. They want to understand. They need the familiar. We were told that we were now Americans and could only speak English, which we did not know. I remember crying when I heard someone speak Flemish. Don't deprive traumatized children of their language…they need to be able to communicate with a language that has feelings that they can understand attached to the spoken words.

If these children need to leave their country, provide them with as many familiar sounds, sites, and smells as possible. They can learn a new language while continuing to speak their native language at home if possible. If no one around them now speaks their native language, find other ways to communicate. Don't wait until the child is fluent in their new language.

Many children may appear normal at first and look as though they are taking everything in their stride. Some of these youngsters may develop generalized anxiety, panic disorders, major depressions, physical illness or somatic symptoms. They may be hyper-aroused by loud sounds, cry as they experience flashbacks, and even have serious sleep disturbances. They may be silent when it comes to these symptoms, giving the impression that all is well with them. Many children are afraid to fall asleep as they are plagued by nightmares. If they do fall asleep, they wake up repeatedly. They can be helped through all of this pain, but they need opportunities to talk about their experiences and hopefully put the past to rest.

Simple events that the average American takes in stride were difficult for us. Johnnie took Corrie to a fourth of July fireworks display that most people love. She started screaming hysterically with the first bang, and wasn't able to stop until she got back to our home. She heard bombs, not fireworks, and her fear stayed with her. Once more, it was quite a while before she could sleep. I had felt jealous that I couldn't go, but when I saw Corrie when they returned, I was glad I hadn't.

Most people don't pay attention to the planes that are constantly flying overhead. We, however, initially got down under our desks, or tended to freeze and stare at the sky. We were afraid. Planes, for us, still meant bombs. We were told to stop being silly. Our fear stayed with us. No one helped us understand what our panic was about.

I suffered many of the symptoms described above and when I saw a doctor, he assumed I was making things up. He never asked about my history. PTSD was not something he considered as it was not yet in the diagnostic manual. All three of us girls have dealt with chronic pain. My sister, Ria, had issues with substance abuse for most of her life. Corrie and I got a good deal of psychotherapy, and it was incredibly helpful. Ria chose not to get psychiatric help. Had help come to us shortly after the war, perhaps we could have avoided some of our pathological responses which added to our pain.

To deal with PTSD, the child must have information available with respect to what happened and must confront her vulnerability during wartime. With new information, she can learn that her world is not as dangerous now as during the war. Slowly, she can learn new coping skills, stop globally avoiding or dwelling on memories of the war, and gain mastery over her feelings. She can explore the decisions she made during these stressful times and redecide those that are not helpful.

Violent traumatic experiences charge the body with adrenaline which can be addictive. Any kind of excitement floods the body with hormones. It does not matter if the events are good or bad. People sometimes crave this charged state and even produce experiences which will provide a new charge. Drugs and alcohol are the vehicles some people use to provide the charge or some look at the sedative effects of these chemicals. "They might help me forget." For some individuals in pain, blotting out sensation is preferable to experiencing it. Some individuals may choose to hurt themselves in order to feel mastery over past traumatic experiences. This is an issue that must be dealt with or the child could develop long-term depression, psychosomatic complaints, continue sleep disturbances, seek out alcohol, drugs or unsafe experiences to produce this high or this low.

Children of war must get psychological help as soon as possible. Many of the issues that become lifelong problems can be put in the past with early intervention. Putting trauma into the past does not mean forgetting the event completely. It does mean that when the event is remembered, the memory does not include the pain and fear that accompanied the historical experience.

Learning how to express oneself and how to verbalize feelings are critical to gaining mastery. Taking in permission to express feelings about past events and get comfort while doing so helps to reduce the pain. It is important that past experiences be heard and acknowledged. Talking about the past is very useful. Silence does not help. Many families grew up with a code of silence when it came to the war. Children and grandchildren of survivors of war are often very reluctant to ask any questions relating to war experiences. They often do this out of sensitivity, and fear, stirring up terrible memories. Once this code of silence is broken, it is amazing how healing it is to share this previously unmentionable pain.

Mom and Kristy 1977

Kristy 1979 Australia

226

Corrie

My Children 1981

www.ingramcontent.com/pod-product-compliance
Lightning Source LLC
Chambersburg PA
CBHW061134160726
48006CB00037B/2014